ALEKSANDR BLOK

NINA BERBEROVA

Aleksandr Blok: A Life

translated from the French
by ROBYN MARSACK

George Braziller, Inc.
New York

First published in the United States by George Braziller, Inc. in 1996

Originally published in 1996 by Carcanet Press Limited,
Britain and by Alyscamps Press, France.

English translation copyright © 1996 by Robyn Marsack
Translated from the French, *Alexandre Blok et son temps*,
copyright © 1991 by Actes Sud, Arles.

For information, please address the publisher:
George Braziller, Inc.
171 Madison Avenue
New York, NY 10016

Library of Congress Cataloging-in-Publication Data:

Berberova, Nina Nikolaevna.
  [Alexandre Blok et son temps. English]
  Aleksandr Blok : a life / Nina Berberova ; translated from the
French by Robyn Marsack.
      p.   cm.
  ISBN 0-8076-1408-4 (hardcover)
    1. Blok, Aleksandr Aleksandrovich, 1880–1921—Biography.
2. Poets, Russian—20th century—Biography.   I. Title.
PG3453.B6Z62513   1996
891.71'3—dc20
  [B]   96-17053
                                                        CIP

Set in 12/13.5pt Apollo by XL Publishing Services, Nairn,
Printed and bound in England by SRP Ltd, Exeter

FIRST EDITION

Ah, if you only knew, children,
The cold and shadows of the days to come!

ALEKSANDR BLOK
27 February 1914

I

The Neva is broad and blue, the sea is near by. It was this river that determined Peter the Great's decision: a city must be born there. He gave it his own name.

But the Neva does not always stay blue. Often it is grey and black, and then – for six months of the year – frozen. In spring its ice, several metres thick, and the ice from Lake Ladoga melt and rush towards the sea in gigantic blocks. In autumn the wind blows, mist covers the city – the most premeditated city in the world.

Dostoevsky said, 'In this mist, a strange, obsessive thought has occurred to me a hundred times: what if, one day, this fog should lift and disappear? Might not this rotting, sticky town disappear too, might it not rise with this fog and dissolve like smoke? Only the old marsh would remain and, in its midst, to make it more enticing, the Bronze Horseman would be set up on a panting, foam-flecked horse. He to whom all this had appeared in a dream would suddenly wake up, and nothing would be left!' Then the nordic horizon would return to its humble flatness; along the silent canals a Karelian fisherman, his face unreadable, would once more cast his line, as in the seventeenth century, before Peter the Great caused all the commotion.

That commotion might have begun a century earlier. It looked as though the Gudunov dynasty would lead Russia along the road taken by the peoples of Europe. But the people did not want the Gudunovs; they cut the throat of Fyodor – young, handsome, intelligent, cultivated. Neither a legend nor a song celebrates him. Even the whereabouts of his tomb is unknown. And when Peter the Great came along, everything was still to be done. Russia lagged a century behind.

He was everywhere at once, never stopping to consider

the consequences of his thoughts and actions. He was constantly creating things: raising towns, marking out roads, building a fleet. He adopted a little black African, an orphan and prisoner of the Turks: the great-grandfather of Pushkin. Thus Peter the Great gave Russia St Petersburg and Pushkin, the two sources of Russian poetry.

In summer, on the broad blue Neva – six times wider than the Seine – little boats plied between the Academy of Medicine and the Academy of Sciences, and the great Mendeleyev, who established the Periodic Table, took them when he visited Professor Borodin, the eminent chemist, who was composing *Prince Igor* in his spare time.

University life was concentrated along the river banks. No other capital had so many institutions ranked side by side along its quays: academies of sciences, of fine arts, of medicine, the university, the Institute of Philology, the Institute of Engineering, the Marine Academy. Of course there were other important districts, and other circles, but they were of no interest either to the botanist Beketov, or to Butlerov, members of all the European academies. For them the great event of the year was the arrival of a scientist from Heidelberg at the St Petersburg Academy, or a recent discovery by Pasteur in distant Paris. In their vast, comfortable houses, in their peaceful libraries crammed with books, in their up-to-date laboratories, the scientists worked intensely for the glory of emergent Russian science.

Their emancipated wives had active personal lives; despite their numerous offspring they read the Goncourts, translated Balzac and de Vigny, and worked for the reform of women's institutions. Their well-informed and well-educated daughters travelled abroad, appreciated Liszt and Berlioz, loved the world and, once a week, invited their fathers' students to dances.

These evenings were lively and gay. The old professors, with their long hair and beards and long black frock-coats, played cards. Around the samovar, the women's conversation darted from literature to teaching to everyday life. The young men, budding scholars – some still awkward, others already worldly – waltzed with the wasp-waisted young ladies who, for the most part, already preferred Stendhal to Chateaubriand.

Such were the receptions at Professor Beketov's. He was Rector of the university, and lived in a large university apartment with tall windows opening on to the Neva. On winter evenings the *izvostchiks* (cab-drivers) in their grimy sheepskin vests, their top-hats gleaming, whipped the little horses bringing the guests. The suppers were simple: tea and sandwiches. The eldest of his daughters was engaged. The third, Aleksandra, was only seventeen. Vivacious, nervous, mischievous, rather ugly, with a bright mind and already serious tastes, she was a cherished little devil. Her father, professor of botany, and her mother, translator of French novels, had taught her to love what was true. She wrote poetry. On her bedside table she had Daudet's tales and, hidden under her pillow, *L'Education sentimentale*.

She was already drawn to complicated things, more so than her mother and sisters. She was courted, but the young men in her circle were nothing more than comrades to her. She was waiting for a genius, and it wasn't long before he arrived.

It was during the winter of 1877 that the young law graduate Aleksandr Lvovich Blok was presented to the Beketovs. His mother was Russian, of the old landed nobility; his father was of German origin. Lithe, handsome, with sad eyes and a bitter smile, he bore all the marks of the *fin-de-siècle*. Despite his vigour, there was something unhealthy about him. The constant analysis of his thoughts and actions paralysed his intentions and threw him into perpetual turmoil. He was enormously knowledgeable about literary, historical and philosophical matters, but he lacked the creative force of real talent. One desire tormented him: he was searching for a new form for his philosophical and sociological writings, a concise style that did not exist, and he was wearing himself out in the endeavour to invent it. He knew nothing of the happy medium; only extremes attracted him. His loves were tinged with hate, he struggled to negate the values he adored. His manias and eccentricities were not yet apparent. He passed his Master's examination brilliantly, and was offered a chair at Warsaw University.

This intelligent, paradoxical man, both cold and passionate, well-read and an excellent musician, made a deep impression on the Beketovs. He had nothing in common with their usual guests, the agreeable dancers who entertained the young ladies or the elderly professors who, charmingly unaware of contradictions, mixed their positivist and revolutionary discoveries with the old religious, familial and idealist traditions. Blok was a 'new man'.

When Aleksandra realized that he loved her, she was flattered and astonished. He asked for her hand: she refused, unable to believe that she could make such a man happy. He stopped coming to the house, and she felt his absence painfully. She understood how much she had enjoyed the bright repartee, the irony, the paradoxes, the rigorous intellect and lively intelligence of young Blok. When he returned, she displayed such charm that he was taken by surprise. They talked things over; their engagement was announced and soon the favourite daughter, the soul of the old house, went away.

The tall windows, from which so much could be seen – pleasure-steamers, small boats, launches, yachts – and in front of which Aleksandra, laughing and mischievous, used to dance and sing, living like a bird, thanking God for life: those windows were closed. The anxious father plunged into his herbals and said nothing; the mother, the old nurse and the little sister impatiently waited for news from Warsaw. Letters were short and infrequent: Aleksandra was happy; she was expecting a baby, but the infant was stillborn; she wanted another child.

Life in Warsaw profoundly changed the young woman. Her imagination and sensibility, her fervent desire for a free and carefree life had ill-prepared her for Blok's difficult character as a husband: jealous, cruel, taciturn, capricious, he loved her not as a wife but as a victim, to be treated as the whim took him. Evening after evening in their apartment in a sombre Warsaw suburb, the servants dismissed, doors and windows shut tight, he ground her down in an agony of which she was not fully aware at the time. He often raised his hand to strike her. He would not allow her to have friends or personal opinions; he wanted to be her universe. Some days, some nights, his passion and his understanding led to a lull which made her happy and confident again. But a trifle would provoke atrocious scenes. His voice would rise, menacingly, his gaze harden, and he would shower her with abuse. She was terror-stricken. Her eighteen years, this solitude which she could not get used to, this unknown city, this strange man who inspired indescribable fear – all of it rendered her defenceless. Two years rolled by, in tears.

In the spring of 1880 they returned to Petersburg. She was pregnant, scarcely recognizable.

Blok defended his thesis in the viva voce examination with resounding success, and completed his work, *Power and European Society*. He was the first sociologist in Russia to deal with the class struggle.

The Beketovs were opposed to Aleksandra's travelling back; he protested but the family stood firm. He returned to Warsaw alone.

Numerous legends lurked about Aleksandr Lvovich (Uncle Sacha, as we called him). As children we were scared of meeting him. Before I knew him, I'd heard that he lived far away in Warsaw, alone, in a dirty, strangely furnished flat. Two wives had left him already; he used to beat them. One of them had just escaped having her throat slit. He had also tortured his children, but they had been taken away.

His photograph was in the album: very handsome, still young, his eyes cruel, his head lowered with a taciturn air; all this corresponded perfectly with the stories of Warsaw, the lonely flat and the knife he'd held one day at the throat of one of his wives.

The first time I saw him he no longer had that demonic, authoritative air. He wasn't very tall but thin and stooped, with thin hair and a thin beard. He lingered in a dark corner and didn't like strangers. At table he was very quiet. If he did venture a few words, he would laugh in confusion – a forced, sardonic laugh...

One day I went to visit him in Warsaw. He was seated on a divan next to a table. He advised me to keep on my overcoat as it was very cold in the flat. He never lit a fire. There was no maid; a cleaning woman came in occasionally. He took his meals in cheap restaurants. At home he drank only tea. He was extremely economical in his movements – it was a fixation with him – and explained to me:

'In the cupboard there I keep the sugar-bowl; when I make tea in the evening, after work, I put away the inkwell and in the same movement take down the sugar-bowl. And in the morning, I put away the sugar and take out my inkwell.'

He was unkempt. I have never seen such dirty, frayed cuffs as his, yet he spent a lot of time washing himself, with those same economical movements. He had placed an armchair in the bathroom.

'I wash my hands, then I sit down and I think,' he said.*

*From the *Memoirs* of Georges Blok.

II

On 16 November 1880 (28 November in the new calendar) in St Petersburg, Aleksandra, separated for ever from her husband, gave birth to Aleksandr Aleksandrovich Blok.

Around him were his grandmother, great-grandmother, mother, aunts, nurse: boundless adoration, too much adoration, verging on idolatry!

When he cried, Professor Beketov took him in his arms and carried him right through the house to show him the boats on the river. All his life he retained a sort of mystical love of boats. His grandfather was his first friend: together they played at bandits, turning the house upside down, and in summer they went for walks which lengthened with each year. They returned grubby and ravenous, but bearing triumphantly some extraordinary violet or rare fern.

The old professors marvelled at his precocious intelligence and his beauty. Mendeleyev introduced him to his daughter, a year younger. All along the quays passers-by turned round to admire the two beautiful children walking with their nannies.

How charming he looks in his early photographs, with his fine features and large eyes, his blond hair falling over the wide lace collar! At five he was a chatterbox and composed his first poems.

> Nice little rabbit, little grey rabbit,
> I love you.
> For you, in the kitchen garden
> I pick cabbages.

And:

> Once upon a time there was a nice little cat
> Who was always sad.

Why? No one knew.
The little cat did not say why.

Big dogs, hedgehogs, lizards – all animals were his friends. He did not know what an enemy was: everyone around him was good to him. But the dearest of all was his mother.

The secret bond between them was never broken. In the reciprocal love of Blok and his mother there was constant anxiety, painful concern. For a long time she was his best adviser, his closest friend. It was she who, consciously and unconsciously, gave him the urge to write. Wishing to provide her son with a father, when Blok was nine years old she married again, Lieutenant Frants Feliksovich Kublitsky-Piottukh.

This small, nervous woman, who suffered from a heart condition and was in love with the ideal, found no happiness in love. Her real gifts were never developed. Her only hope of escape from nothingness was her son. He kept coming back to her, as to a touchstone, because he owed to her the unclouded happiness of his childhood.

But for the moment life was made up of games, walks, fairy-tales. He gathered around himself everything he loved: dogs, boats he sailed on the lake, glue, cardboard, paper for binding his books or making boats.

His father came to see him once a year; neither of them had anything to say to the other. Anyway Blok was becoming less and less talkative. They wanted him to learn French, but he spoke so little to his French governess that she was dismissed.

It was during the summer months, on the estate at Shakhmatovo, that he was happiest. This was not one of those 'nests of gentlefolk' where the great nineteenth-century writers lived. It was no more than a modest house in the middle of a large garden; Professor Beketov had bought it to be near his friend Mendeleyev, and it later belonged to Blok. Halfway between Petersburg and Moscow, surrounded by vast woods belonging to the State, the house was hidden behind centuries-old lime-trees. An avenue of firs led to the lake; everywhere there was a jumble of old trees, jasmine, lilac and wild roses, which they preferred to the order of an 'English' garden. It was there that Blok learned to walk, to talk, to read, to love animals. It was there, too, that he developed a taste for writing. 'I remember the waves of lyricism which, while I was still a child, used to engulf me there,' he wrote later.

The old horse, which he drove himself, took the family to the station. They returned to Petersburg, to the Kublitskys' new flat, far away in the Imperial Grenadier Barracks, near the botanical gardens. Here the river was narrower, the quays were not so grand. But there were still boats, working cranes, small craft at their moorings. The high school was near by. His studies began; friends and cousins came to join him.

Several years passed, and we find Blok at fourteen the chief editor of *The Messenger*, a journal produced in one copy. Grandmother contributed poems, his mother stories; Grandfather did the illustrations. Uncles and aunts and everyone joined in. The whole family was absorbed in literature; cousins entered the fray, and Blok began to compose his first real poems: epigrams, satires on family life and sentimental verses dedicated mainly to his mother, speaking of moonlight and the beauties of spring at Shakhmatovo. They were all fairly mediocre efforts.

When he was sixteen, he discovered the theatre, and this discovery was utterly overwhelming. He went to the classical matinées, performances of Griboyedov, Molière, Shakespeare. His main enthusiasm was for Shakespeare, for the violence of his passions and his wealth of imagination. He wanted to act. Everywhere, in front of anyone who would watch and listen, he declaimed the soliloquies from *Macbeth* and *Hamlet*. His mind was made up: he would be an actor.

In 1897 he went with his mother to Bad Neuheim, a German spa town. Madame Kublitskaya was suffering from heart pains and nervous symptoms that would later grow worse.

Blok was seventeen. He was a very handsome boy, thoughtful and quiet, who declaimed in the old-fashioned manner the poems of Maykov and Fet, who dreamed of playing *Hamlet* on the real stage, who was – like most of his friends – still childlike and already a bit of a dandy. He didn't have the enormous curiosity and hunger for knowledge peculiar to adolescence. Indeed he never had a great thirst for reading; other people's thoughts didn't interest him much. Only his own feelings, his own ideas and reactions are stamped on his work.

He met Xenia Sadovskaya, a very beautiful married woman, ten years his senior. And in that worldly, pleasant little town, free of obligations and constraints, he experienced his first love affair. An untroubled love, tender, charming, fresh and youthful, the memory of which is preserved in poems of an eclectically romantic style, poems that are neither striking nor individual.

The lovers met again in Petersburg; then their meetings became less frequent and, imperceptibly, they drifted apart. Blok, however, never quite forgot the first awakenings of his feelings. Twelve years later he wrote:

> What did youth and tenderness, what
> did they mean to both of us?
> Surely they're behind the dark
> impetuosity of this verse?

And again:

> Life has been burnt up, it's a tale that's told;
> I can see nothing but my first love,
> like a casket that's been knotted
> with a ribbon that's as bright as my blood.

III

At the end of the nineteenth century no purely literary grouping existed in Russia, no group had been formed to defend and illustrate a new aesthetic. The great writers of the period didn't belong to any school. After the *pléaide* of the 1820s–1840s, Pushkin's era, the first group to demonstrate a sort of community of effort, to establish a real literary school, were the Russian Symbolists. Despite all their differences, Russian Symbolism may be regarded as the collective creation of a fairly homogenous group.

Who were the great poets of the period? Fet, the last romantic, born in 1820, was dead. Maykov, the last of the classical poets, died in 1897. Around 1890, at the time generally described as that of 'political reaction', Russian literature was dominated by a naive, 'civic' tendency. This broke with the great Russian poetic tradition of Pushkin, Tyutchev and Lermontov, indeed dismissed it. Gogol remained misunderstood; Dostoevsky was not only misunderstood but for the most part rejected. It was Nekrasov, who had died in 1877, who had pushed poetry down this road, into a cul-de-sac: political themes, revolt against the regime, love of the poor. Thus Nekrasov occupied first place and his influence prevailed against Pushkin's. The writer was required to serve the social interest. The novelist had to paint the lives of his heroes and their background with the utmost precision and detail, and play his part in resolving political and social problems. Poets were expected to produce compassionate verses about their 'suffering brothers' or the struggle for a 'better future'. Nekrasov's formula, 'You may not be able to be a poet, / But you have to be a citizen' was invoked at every turn, whether appropriate or not.

This 'civic' tendency had a deep psychological basis and

demonstrated indisputable moral qualities. On the other hand, its aesthetic ideas were few and far between. Thus Russian criticism resolutely separated form from content. Only the subject was considered important; moreover, there were very severe rules. Individualism and religion were as rigorously rooted out by liberal criticism as atheism was by government censorship. Form played no more than a modest, auxiliary part. Indeed the question of form was not even raised with regard to prose. In poetry, the only requirements were to observe the most elementary rules of prosody. All complexity was regarded as superfluous dandyism, and efforts to achieve formal perfection, far from being looked on sympathetically, were denounced as reactionary, a shameful betrayal of the 'common cause'.

Those who did not accept the ideal of 'citizen', who wanted to be poets, took refuge in philosophy larded with capital letters, in gypsy romances or in sterile imitations of the classics. And these years, when the novels of the great Russian writers had their unique triumph, when each line by Tolstoy was an event and when Chekhov reached the pinnacle of his glory, were years without poetry.

Among the philosophical poets, one stood out: Vladimir Solovev. His emphatic line of argument is alien to us now. Equally inspired by the great religious philosophers of the West and by the gnostics and mystics of the East, drawing on the Vedas, Goethe and the Apocalypse, he is better to read in prose than in poetry, and perhaps should be considered as a thinker rather than a poet. He was the only one of his generation to turn towards those things which his contemporaries did not regard as part of 'actuality'.

Protestations against the poverty and monotony of ideas, against the mediocre style of the 'citizen poets' were inevitable, and they came from the poets themselves. Literature had to move towards freeing itself from the surveillance of the publicists and to rediscover its independence. Like a bell sounding the tocsin, French Symbolism gave the signal for revolt and provided the first slogan, heard simultaneously in Moscow and St Petersburg: *De la musique avant toute chose.*

The line became a sacred commandment for the man who proclaimed the renaissance of Russian poetry and founded a school which, in the first flush of his literary enthusiasm, he baptised 'Russian Symbolism'. This was Valery Bryusov, who was only a schoolboy at the time. His whole 'school' was made up of two or three young men with whom he read Verlaine, Baudelaire, Mallarmé. Soon Konstantin Balmont joined Bryusov, and the two attracted other disciples.

Independently of Moscow, and almost simultaneously, the literary revolution broke out in St Petersburg. Zinaida Gippius and Dmitry Merezhkovsky gave the watchword. An exchange of echoes, a sort of mutual attraction was soon established between Moscow and Petersburg. It should be noted, however, that this attraction by no means indicated that they completely understood each other, especially as the positive aims and slogans for the struggle hadn't yet been laid down by either group. They weren't clear even to the revolutionaries themselves. Only their common enemies were obvious. The alliance between Moscow and Petersburg was more tactical than ideological, and did not rest on any precise agreement. Later, the two groups spent their literary lives both trying to get to know each other and trying to create their own identities. Although they were constantly attracted to each other, they were equally desirous of being separate, moving from love to hate, fighting within the very heart of the alliance without ever actually breaking it.

It frequently happens that our struggles make us a sort of mirror image of our enemies. In opposing the injustices of our enemies, we often elevate above the truth principles so diametrically opposite that they, in their turn, are merely new errors – not the same as the errors we are opposing, but errors none the less.

The dominant literature at the time symbolism was emerging, and that Bryusov and Balmont were fighting against, separated form from content and considered the first unimportant. But by the formula *De la musique avant toute chose*, Balmont and Bryusov did not mean simply the opposite principle. They did not proclaim the predominance of form over content; it was just that they did not know how to describe exactly the kind of poetry they had in mind. They wanted form to play more than an auxiliary part; it was in working at form, cultivating form, that they found their chief impetus, the main dynamic factor of their poetry. This was easier in that neither Balmont nor Bryusov had positive philosophical, religious or social ideas. Their ideas were purely literary, strictly formal, and their poetic activity was basically formal. If anyone had asked Bryusov what he wanted, he would have replied in all conscience, 'I want to make poems. – About what? It's all the same to me.' This is essentially what he's saying in what became his famous lines:

> It may be that life is only a means
> For the creation of melodious, vivid verses;
> So from your carefree childhood,
> Search for combinations of words.

In the absence of ideas, emotions have to furnish the themes of poetry; this is what led the Muscovite Symbolists to extreme individualism, which they called the cult of personality. While a new poetic form did not arise out of their individualism, individualism was required to nourish a new form. According to one contemporary, a 'fevered race for any and every emotion' then began. All sensations were regarded as worthwhile, just as long as they were numerous, strong and novel. Thus personality became a sack, and all emotional moments were crammed into it indiscriminately. He who accumulated the most was considered the richest and most remarkable being. In this 'race' some creative energy was dispersed without taking poetic form, and the moments passed, leaving the soul exhausted and empty. The 'greedy cavaliers' of Muscovite symbolism expired of inner hunger, of spiritual usury, on the sacks of jealously accumulated sensations. It wasn't only their souls that died. The school was noted for a striking series of suicides amongst the disciples and victims of Bryusov. It has even been said that Bryusov died on the eve of committing suicide. 'We ourselves have fallen in a holocaust on the altar of poetry,' he wrote in one of his manifestos.

In Petersburg the poetic revolution took the opposite path. It offered new content rather than new form. The theme of religion, considered reactionary and therefore forbidden by liberal critics, had become Merezhkovsky's theme. He linked the problems of history, politics, social life and literature to those of religion and the Church. Ancient themes appeared in a new guise; he showed them from a previously unexplored angle. Merezhkovsky's point of view was opposed to the Church's, on the one hand, and to the social positivists' on the other. This disagreement lasted over thirty years and often took dramatic forms; moreover, it coincided with troubled years in Russia's history. In this period Merezhkovsky, it must be said, revealed himself as one of the writers most immersed in ideas. He exercised enormous influence, not only over his disciples but also over his opponents and those who distanced themselves from the problems he raised. He worked at educating the critic and the reader, trying to accustom them to approach Russian literature from a philosophical, profound point of view. After Dostoevsky's lecture on Pushkin, Merezhkovsky was the first to take up the topic of the meaning and prophetic weight of Russian literature, suggesting a new way of considering the works of Dostoevsky, Tolstoy, Gogol and Lermontov.

The philosopher in Merezhkovsky, however, soon crushed the artist. In his poetry – which he soon gave up writing – as in his novels, everything tended towards the religious rather than the aesthetic. His novels had no heroes, only the clash of thesis and antithesis. Impregnated with new ideas, Merezhkovsky's novels were simply *romans-à-these*, and in that resembled the works which had provoked the birth of Symbolism. Revolutionary in content, they were no more concerned with form than were the representatives of the 'civic' tendency.

'We have too many works of art,' he said, 'and not

enough criticism.' For an artist, there can never be 'too many works of art'.

Zinaida Gippius was never actually a disciple of Merezhkovsky. Her writings are imbued with a particular and deeply individual character. But as her own ideas were close to his, she always faithfully followed him. Their alliance was primarily based on a shared attitude to the problematic relationship of form to content. If Zinaida Gippius was able to write a number of good poems, she owed it to an unconscious guiding poetic instinct. Yet her stories, novels and plays were at least as tendentious as those of Merezhkovsky. Her penchant for polemic, springing from a wish to follow all differences of opinion to their limits, took her even further. She tried to suppress all signs of artistry, to the extent that their very absence constituted a new method. In her essays she refused to take into consideration the form of the work she was analysing, but severely interrogated the author as to his faith.

The Moscow school and the Petersburg school had inherited the original sin of their predecessors, the separation of form and matter. The first, indifferent to all ideology, sought new forms. The second, dismissing form, was hungry for ideas. This divergence determined their inmost attitudes as well. When Gippius questioned Bryusov about his religious belief, he replied:

> In intangible truth
> I've had no faith for a long time.
> All seas, all ports
> I love with an equal love.
> I wish only to sail
> My free skiff everywhere.
> And I want to sing the praises
> Of the Lord along with Satan's.

And Balmont:

> They make no sense to me, your exclamations:
> Christ, Anti-Christ, Satan, Lord!

I am the murmur of blossoming,
I am the breath of the zephyr.

In response, Merezhkovsky called Balmont a rattlebox. The two parties were both right and wrong, but they jealously guarded their positions.

IV

Impersonal, bland, often banal, Blok's adolescent poems hold little interest. His ideas about poetry were very confused. The future elements of his work, his ideas and his premonitions of form were slowly taking shape but everything rattled about, pulled this way and that without becoming fixed.

In about 1898 one element began to predominate: the Eternal Feminine sought incarnation in his poetry, not as the object of dawning love but as the meaning and end of the Universe. At the same time, Blok discovered the poetry of Vladimir Solovev, that poetry springing wholly from the Eternal Feminine. Apocalyptic, heavily charged with Meaning, far too influenced by the second part of *Faust*, grandiloquent – this poetry is far from today's taste. But Blok was overwhelmed on reading it, and it suddenly crystallized what had been obscurely disturbing him.

> My family and its traditions, a fairly restricted life, meant that I did not know a single line of modern poetry until my entry into university. Thus Solovev's poetry filled my being, closely responding to my feelings of mysticism and romanticism. Until then, the mysticism of the last years of the century had been incomprehensible. The signs I had perceived all around had worried me, but I believed that I was the only one to notice them and I hid my anxiety.

While he didn't become a disciple of the poet, whose form did not satisfy him, Blok genuinely adored Solovev. The engaging personality of the man – whom he met once – and his extraordinary life filled Blok with wonder.

Yet at this period he was still bent on the theatre. On stage, however, he didn't act: he declaimed. He recited Hamlet's soliloquy, clinging to the poetry and the music of

18

the words without living the part. His friends encouraged him, seduced by his beauty, his graceful figure, his warm, solemn voice, his romantic air and charming manner.

Dmitry Ivanovich Mendeleyev, whose estate lay not far from Shakhmatovo, often visited the Beketovs. Grandfather Beketov, now very old, had had a heart attack. Ringing through the house came the loud voice of Mendeleyev, large, long-haired and boisterous, his head always full of new projects. One day he invited Blok to join all the young people at his house. When Blok was five, he had gone for walks with the older daughter. Like him, she had been born in Petersburg, in a university building.

He arrived at Boblovo on horseback one afternoon. With his tall boots, embroidered shirt, his luxuriant blond hair and grave expression, he made a proud figure. Lyubov and Mademoiselle received him. His beauty and especially his plans to stage Labiche and Shakespeare in the barn carried everyone along. Lyubov said nothing; she was most reserved and difficult to approach. Very beautiful, tall, with long golden hair, grey eyes and black eyebrows, and a pink-and-white complexion, she was more of a Valkyrie than an Ophelia. Nevertheless, she was very successful in the mad scene!

Blok returned often, always something of the young Tsar Ivan, the legendary prince come to find his Lady. Young, supple and severe, she combed her long tresses in the sunshine.

Solovev's lines sang in his head, prophetically:

> Know that here, descended to earth,
> Is the Eternal Feminine in flesh incorruptible.

Blue and gold, *She* appeared in the work of both poets. It was only after Solovev's death, in July 1900, that in Blok's *She* took on the character of Sophia, of Wisdom, eternally young. He awaited her; *ante lucem*, full of inner light. He saw her and lived passionately in the meeting. Then, *post lucem*, he remained prostrate over the traces of her foot-steps. (The poems written before the daily visits to the

Mendeleyevs bear the note *ante lucem*; those written afterwards, the note *post lucem*.)

The young girl, the fairy-tale princess, Wisdom, gradually became this World Soul, the woman clothed with the sun.* Apocalypse was inherent in his life. The form of apocalyptic thought became his ultimate form. Twenty years later, he would define what Solovev had been to him in those years: 'Destiny had made Solovev throughout his life the bearer of ideas and prophet of events which he had to unfold to the world... Each of us felt that the end of events was still not upon us and that it was impossible to predict.'

He didn't speak about his feelings to anyone except his mother, who entirely shared his enthusiasm for Solovev's poetry. Her cousin had married the thinker's brother, Mikhail Sergeyevich Solovev; she introduced them to Blok. Extremely intelligent, discriminating and cultivated, Mikhail Solovev and his wife were sensitive to everything young and new. Their son, Sergey, five years younger than Blok, was already very gifted and knowledgeable. He had been writing poetry since he was twelve and his parents believed that they recognized in him the spiritual heir of Vladimir Solovev. As children he and Blok had played in the woods of Shakhmatovo; one day, beneath the ancient elms, they had celebrated mass. When they met again in the summer of 1900, they discussed their ideas about poetry and read their poems to each other. Blok was writing a great deal. In a big notebook, which he headed with two lines from Pushkin –

> He had one vision only,
> Which reason could not comprehend,

– he wrote his first poems to the Beautiful Lady.

Lyubov was there again, in the tall, solid residence Mendeleyev had built, and in which he carried out his extraordinary experiments. Proud and severe, she waited for Blok without any show of impatience. An oak-tree, more

---

*Revelations 12:1. (Revelations is *L'Apocalypse* in French – Trs.)

than three hundred years old, hid the tall narrow window where she plaited her long hair.

They were still passionate about the theatre, and Shakespeare haunted them more than ever. Blok resumed the costume of the Prince of Denmark, and we see the cap, the pen and the knot entering his poems. Lyubov makes her entrance, too, in Ophelia's song, which he arranged for her — her wreath of flowers, her mad smile.

'My lyric poems, from 1897, can be read as an intimate diary,' he was to say later.

Thus he showed his love for this solemn, haughty young woman.

'I remember my trips to Boblovo, on horseback, on foot, the dark nights, the bushes full of glow-worms, Lyubov's severity.'

Like him, she gazed from an open window at the break of dawn, the dawn of a new century, announced in summer storms, forest fires, the flight of a comet and a shower of stars at the beginning of autumn.

The next winter he wrote numerous poems for her. He met her at the theatre. Salvini was playing Lear. Shakespeare was certainly propitious for their encounters. Blok had changed, filled out, was reading much more and talking less. From time to time the memory of Xenia, whom he still saw occasionally, came back to him. He wanted to put an end to that story. Twenty years later he wrote: '*She* was beginning to take on aspects of reality.'

January 1901: from this date, for three years, Blok abandoned himself unreservedly to mysticism, to love, to poetry. The poet expanded, became aware of his art; his work gained in power, in richness, in beauty; the magnificent *Verses to the Most Beautiful Lady* were born. And for three years Russian poetry knew a purity, a loftiness, a charm rarely equalled.

25 January – walk down Monetny Street. Evening. A strange sensation. At the end of January and beginning of February, *She* actually appeared. She who was living became the World

Soul (as I later understood), the Soul separated, imprisoned, languishing... I could only look on her and bless her...

In this state of mind, he met Lyubov. She was on her way to a lecture; he followed her. He never took his eyes off her along the streets of Vasilyevsky Island. The next day, he retraced his steps. Then he went further, beyond the island, towards the mouth of the river, towards the Old Town. The sun was setting in the sea; the sunsets were red, the nights clear and short. Dawn found him wandering, interpreting the signs of sky and earth.

In May I tried on 'internal armour' for the first time, to protect myself from her severity with secret knowledge. It was the beginning of 'future sorcery' and of my extraordinary fusion with nature.

It began like this: the feeling of love had become less important than a higher vocation, but the object of both is always the same being. In the first poem written at Shakhmatovo, this being takes on the odd character of the 'Russian Venus'. Afterwards come the amazingly significant 'sorceries' and also the premonition that she could *change her appearance...*

September... Lyuba has become completely indifferent once more. In October, my crises of despair reoccur...

In November 'overt sorcery' begins, because I invoked doubles...

The crowd has taught me to adore Beauty...

I have encountered her; her external aspect in perfect harmony with her superterrestrial aspect, has raised in me a storm of happiness, and makes me understand that this lightsome shadow has brought healing to my sick and deathly soul...

In her earthly form she has come to me, in circumstances that owed nothing to chance, and has given birth not only to prophetic triumph but also to human love. Perhaps I should let her see that because, once again, she has become very severe with me...

And now sunsets are full of visions and bring me tears, fire,
song. Something whispers to me that one day I will return to
the same places, but changed by the terrible laws of Time,
faded, with just any old song (that is as a man, as a poet, but
not as a prophet in possession of a mystery...)

Blok was completely at home with the ideas of Origen, of
Solovev and of Plato, testing a faith which he discussed at
great length with his mother, who understood him better
than anyone else. After this summer filled with poetry and
love, they returned to St Petersburg together. In the train
they came across Sergey's father, to whom Madame
Kublitskaya had sent her son's poems. And Mikhail Solovev
told Blok that his poems had been much appreciated in
Moscow by Boris Bugayev,* a young poet who was Sergey's
friend.

*The real name of Andrey Bely.

V

Son of a famous mathematician, who was Dean of the faculty, Boris Bugayev lived in Moscow, where he had been born the same year as Blok. He had known since 1897 that a young Petersburg cousin of Sergey Solovev – his friend who lived on the same floor – was writing poetry. He also knew that this young man adored Shakespeare and wanted to be an actor. It was Madame Soloveva, a remarkable woman – painter, musician, translator of Ruskin and Wilde – who had spoken to him about Blok. It was also through her that Bugayev had become acquainted with the poetry of Mallarmé and Verlaine. At her house he met Vladimir Solovev shortly before his death. Afterwards she corresponded with Zinaida Gippius. In her salon the early poems of Bryusov and Balmont had been applauded; each book by Merezhkovsky was an event fiercely discussed there.

Bugayev was introduced to the salon by his friend Sergey, then aged twelve. A new world was revealed to him. They read Ben Jonson and Nietzsche; they discussed Russian writers – Pushkin and Tyutchev – as they had never been discussed before in Russia.

When Andrey Bely published his remarkable memoir of Blok, in 1922, he was to define the years 1899 to 1901 as the years 'of dawns'.

> 1898 was the year of grey sky [*Under the Nordic Sky*, poems by Balmont]. The century was coming to an end. 1899 brought mists, 'the mists of consciousness'. 1900–1901 were the years of purification, of azure, of presentiments.

Bely's first volume of poetry was called *Gold on Azure*. 'Let us be like the sun!' said Balmont; and Blok: 'Dawn! Dawn! Dawn!'

A sharp reaction against Schopenhauer and Ibsen set in.

The young, like Sergey and Bely, lived 'all the events of the century as though integral to their own lives'. Dostoevsky was more and more influential and Nietzsche's *Birth of Tragedy* became their new gospel.

The 'old' and 'new' separated irrevocably, like the sea from the land when the world was created. Everything was to be remade. Pessimism developed into tragedy and 'Socratic man' was announced as definitively outmoded.

The new men, who recognized each other at first glance and were sometimes drawn to each other even before being introduced, were more numerous in Moscow than in Petersburg. These 'brothers of the Dawn' saw signs announcing the Light in the great events which set the world on fire and in the little facts of everyday life. As if, after the silence of a century asleep, the footsteps of the coming century could be heard. Contemplation turned into feverish searching, and the symbol of the 'Woman clothed with the sun' was combined with the down-to-earth wisdom of the Gnostics.

In 1901, the little path that led to the cemetery containing Vladimir Solovev's grave became for Sergey and Bely the path of 'Purgatory' and 'Inspiration', and they sought the Universal Soul's incarnation in one of the many young women of Muscovite society. They took it in turns to throw over their shoulders the big pilgrim cape of the beloved philosopher, and both walked the snowy streets bumping into the ghost of Solovev. They looked for his traces in Sergey's parents' estate (not far from Shakhmatovo and Boblovo), where the memory of the dead man was still strong. Mikhail Solovev and his wife encouraged the young men. For the mathematics student Bugayev the pseudonym Andrey Bely – Bely means 'white' in Russian – was chosen, so as not to bring shame on the respected name of his father, Dean in the university.

'At this period,' Bely was to write, 'Blok was the only one who expressed our secret thoughts.' Blok was living ten kilometres away and suspected nothing.

In 1901, Bely took his first steps into literary circles in

Moscow and Petersburg; he met Merezhkovsky, Gippius, Bryusov, Balmont. He and Sergey, with a few friends, founded the 'Argonaut' circle. For these young poets, Symbolism was not only a literary school but also a discipline of life and thought. Unfortunately they lacked someone really talented, a true poet; they tended to be theoreticians and orators who, ardent and audacious, launched into violent polemic.

During the summer of 1901 – so rich in ideas and struggles – Bely received from Sergey Solovev, who was spending his holidays on his parents' estate, a sensational letter: he had renewed acquaintanceship with his cousin, Aleksandr Blok, who, like them, had been struck by Solovev and who sensed Sophia – Wisdom – not as an idea but as an adored woman, close at hand; who, like them, was full of a mysterious, communicative energy.

This letter was a revelation to Bely. When Sergey returned to Moscow in the autumn, Bely extracted from him a dozen of Blok's poems. Everything the Argonauts felt, without being able to express it, everything that bore 'the rose and gold air of the era', everything was there! Blok had set it down in his poetry. He had found 'the luminous Girl from shadowy chaos' (Solovev); he was inviting them to join in her worship.

And for Blok she was indeed alive, and had lately become his fiancée. The poems *To the Most Beautiful Lady* – more than eight hundred of them – were not all published, but, just as Blok wished, they were read as a diary: see her there – beside a lake, at her window, at a street-corner. Her beauty, her purity, her pride began to be familiar to readers. But who was she? The following year, Sergey Solovev revealed her identity to the Argonauts: it was Lyuba, Mendeleyev's daughter, that beautiful, fierce young woman. The members of the 'sect' seized upon the information. '*She* is among us!' they exclaimed. Blok was too absorbed in his love and his poetry to take the 'sect' seriously, unaware that he was its master.

The year 1903 began in tragedy. Mikhail Solovev, acute

and understanding, who encouraged the Argonauts and was the first to give them access to Blok's poems, died; his wife, to whom Bely and others owed so much, killed herself half an hour after her husband's death. Sergey, at eighteen, was alone.

At that moment an extraordinary thing happened: the very same day that Blok wrote to Bely for the first time, Bely sent his first letter to Blok; and thus the two greatest poets of the period made each other's acquaintance.

Blok's poems began to be known in Moscow and Petersburg. In March 1903 they were published simultaneously in Bryusov's review, *Severnye Tsvety* (Northern Flowers) and in Merezhkovsky's *Novyy Put'* (The New Way). The poet was judged by a wider public. There were tough reviews, mocking the *Beautiful Lady*. Nobody understood the 'Dawns'. It all seemed incoherent and pretentious to the petit-bourgeois who had only one word to describe Blok, and Balmont, and Merezhkovsky: decadent.

The wedding-day drew near; Blok's father sent a thousand roubles, which wasn't much. Everything had to be bought: furniture, clothing, rings. His mother helped him with everything. The religious ceremony made a deep impression on Blok. Madame Kublitskaya and old Mendeleyev wept with joy and emotion. The young bride in white batiste and the silent, thoughtful Blok emerged from the chapel. The troika was there; the coachman, in a bright pink shirt and with a feather in his cap, was waiting. The peasants sang in chorus and presented the couple with white geese, bread and salt. Sergey Solovev, who was best man, never forgot this radiant day.

The Beautiful Lady, whose footsteps the poet had so often traced through the city streets, became Madame Aleksandr Blok. He was a student of arts; she was taking a course in the faculty of philology.

VI

Blok and Bely appeared at a critical moment for Russian Symbolism. 'Symbolism', wrote Bely,

> is torn between the truth of human personality, wearing form like armour, and popular truth in the armour of the sermon. Merezhkovsky is all spark and flame, but the direction he is beginning to take leads beyond literature; he does not want Art. Bryusov is all glitter, but what he creates does not give us any notion of what we should be.

Bryusov and Merezhkovsky's positions were thesis and antithesis for the younger men; they had to find a synthesis, a solution to the inner crisis. They wanted neither to resort to a superficial reconciliation of extremes nor to follow the way of simple compromise. They posed the problem of form and content, and resolved it at a deep level. Blok and Bely's mystical vision of the world determined the character of their aesthetic quest and their concept of Symbolism.

Turning towards the poets who had created the golden age of Russian poetry – and in this way following in the footsteps of Solovev and Merezhkovsky – the new Symbolists had recognized in these poets' works fresh proof of the duality of the soul, proof of its double being between existence in time and in eternity. This double being had been defined by Tyutchev better than anyone:

> Oh my prophetic soul,
> Oh heart full of anguish,
> How you flutter on the threshold,
> As it were, of two realities!

The same sort of avowals resound – as well as after Tyutchev – in Lermontov's *Angel* and in Pushkin's efforts to understand 'the obscure language of the night'. One might say that these efforts of prophetic memory constitute the deepest and purest essence of Russian poetry. The poets wanted both to remember this being that partakes of eternity, and to feel its touch once more. Comparing himself to the swallow who flies down to the pond and skims the water with its wing, Fet asked:

> And terror strikes, in case the glassy surface
> Seize the alien element, the flashing wing.
>
> Intrepidity once more – the same dark current!
> Is not inspiration like this –
> And being human, too?[*]

For a poet belonging to the great poetic tradition, this 'dark current' was always the one he most desired and perhaps was the only one that attracted him. 'The element of the beyond' is the native heath of Russian poetry, the land which immediately slips away, which is always sought; even the will to pursue its discovery is, in itself, an infinitely precious national good to the poets of Russia.

What is it and where is it, then, this 'element of the beyond'? It is everywhere and nowhere, in us and beyond us; it is close by and forever escapes us. Everything around us conveys its everlasting memory, is its reflection, its echo. *Alles Vergangliche ist nur ein Gleichniss* (Everything that passes is merely a symbol) – this line by Goethe seems to have risen out of Russian poetry. It also serves as a point of departure for the explorations of the younger generation of Symbolists:

> Dear friend, don't you understand
> That what we see revealed
> Is but a flicker, but a shade
> Of that which is concealed?

asked Vladimir Solovev, their master. To recognize what lasts in the perishable world, the eternal in the temporal, the

---

[*]Translation by James Greene: Afanasy Fet, *I have come to greet you* (London: Angel Books, 1982), p.55.

occult in the visible – this is what the young Symbolists considered to be the essential task of all art.

To carry out this task, what is temporal and knowable by the five senses had to be rediscovered by intuition and absorbed by understanding. Viewed from this angle, artistic creation becomes a transfiguration of reality. Art is not simply the transformation of chaos, which becomes the cosmos, but also a constant metamorphosis, an unceasing recreation.

Temporal reality is present and known to us as a series of images. The artist, seeing them, transforms them into a web of symbols. The symbol is an image changed and illuminated, as it were, by lived experience; it is a form, in as much as it remains an image, but it is also a substance to the extent which it opens, by means of its symbolism, the knowledge of that which is hidden under the surface of things. The birth of a symbol entails the simultaneous birth of a substance inseparable from it. In authentic art, content is inseparable from form; the form is itself the content. The fact that Bely was the first to study rhythm in Russian verse as a science is no chance matter. He noted the rhythmic peculiarities in the same metres used by different poets, and thus discovered a direct link between the rhythmic solution of a poem and its inner dynamics. For Bely, a work of art presents a double aspect: the visible, outer one and the hidden, inner aspect. 'Symbolism is at once classicism, romanticism and realism: it is realism to the extent that it reflects reality; to the extent to which it is an image modified by experience, it is romanticism; and finally, it is classicism, because it provides an alliance of form and substance.'

All art is symbolic – present, past and future art. So what is peculiar to contemporary Symbolism? The Symbolist school is simply intended to unify the statements of artists and poets, affirming that the meaning of beauty resides in the artistic image and not in the simple emotion this image provokes in us, and definitely not in the cerebral explanation of this image. The symbol cannot be broken down into emotions, nor into discursive ideas. The Symbolist school has enlarged the framework of our conception of artistic creation. It has shown that the canon of beauty is not an academic canon: this canon cannot be that of romanticism alone, or of classicism, or of realism. But the Symbolist school has justified the existence of each, in as much as they are aspects of a single creation.

VII

Moscow was waiting for Blok. The Argonauts circulated his poetry and even though Bryusov, the literary man of the moment, remained hostile, Bely felt that the time had come to make Blok known to the Muscovite public.

Balmont, who had made a brilliant debut ten years earlier, saw his star setting. Bryusov was the uncontested master. Disdainful, demonic, proud of his success, he was living through the most glittering years of his career: women, friends, enemies, rivals, disciples! Journals, societies, publishers – all literary life gravitated towards him. He did not recognize in Blok the great poet who would eclipse him to such an extent that his own work would have only historical interest for succeeding generations. He played up to his role as idol and chief, and regarded unfavourably the Argonauts' emancipation, especially that of Bely who was becoming a bit too noisy, making speeches at all the lectures, publishing poems and virulent reviews, and receiving from the quality press a flood of abuse which made him conspicuous.

Since their first exchange of letters, Blok and Bely had been in constant correspondence, which provided a faithful reflection of Blok's state of mind and changed in emphasis over the year. It had begun at the most wonderful period of the poet's life, when he was still totally absorbed by Solovev. He spoke more often of the 'Virgin of the Rainbow' than of Lyuba. One thing puzzled Bely: who exactly was Lyuba? If she were Beatrice, she could not be Blok's wife! And if she were a mere mortal, then he had betrayed the faith. Sergey Solovev said that Lyubov was aware of her 'double role', and that just as Mendeleyev was 'shadowy Chaos', she was indeed 'his Luminous Daughter'.

By the end of 1903 Bely began to tire of the Argonauts

and of all the noisy, futile restlessness which dissipated his energies. He talked a lot and was seen everywhere, but had scarcely any time to write. Sometimes he identified with the sad hero of Griboyedov's play, Repetilov, who when he was asked what he did, replied, 'We make noise, dear chap, we make noise!' From time to time he called a halt and recovered his inner harmony. But soon the relationships, the parades, the rowdy demonstrations, all the hurly burly of literary life, reclaimed him. Disquiet and painful regrets crept up on him; he felt the era of 'Dawns' slipping away...

For Blok, too, that mysterious, marvellous period was far away. After his marriage, the tone of his letters changes. He was working at the faculty, he was writing a lot; his life had become simpler and easier. He was happy. At least, he wanted to be.

Blok considered his weaknesses to be those of the century rather than peculiar to himself. As an adolescent, he had painfully experienced that deep despair which marked his generation, just as boredom had oppressed Chekhov's heroes. This was not part of his romanticism: such despair was of his times, and Blok, like Pushkin, was one with them. His later poems about his native land, in which he foresaw Russia's future or struggled against the presentiment that it would disappear, show the extent to which he lived his times. He carried within himself a poignant sadness, infinite distress, muffled anxiety that the happy days were becoming blurred, distant, but he thought that they would never disappear completely. The beginning of his life with Lyuba, 1903–4, when the severe goddess came to him, were Blok's happiest years. And yet, to what extent was Lyuba his wife? The suspicion that his marriage was only a 'white marriage' throws a curious shadow across this 'happy' period of his life.

But the two of them formed a united and admired couple when, in January 1904, six months after their wedding, they went to Moscow. An elegant young woman, a slender, curly-haired young man, rang the bell of the apartment where Bely lived with his mother. Very 'Petersburg', worldly, a little stiff, Blok was brought into the salon where, gesticulating wildly, jumping up and down, tall and small by turns, Bely rattled on. And the same evening Blok, in a long frock-coat and white gloves, and Lyuba in evening gown, were warmly received by Sergey and the Argonauts. Bryusov and his entourage stared at them curiously. Everyone discussed them; there was great enthusiasm, openly displayed. People in Moscow were quite different from those on the banks of the cold Neva.

After one year's correspondence and two of exchanging poems, Bely immediately became Blok's closest friend, the 'brother'. With Sergey they formed an inseparable trio, sharing Solovev's ideas, a love of modern poetry, and wonder over Lyuba. For the Argonauts, Lyuba was the Universal Soul. Sergey plied her with roses, Bely with lilies. Blok smiled gently, somewhat bemused. They had merry dinners, read poems, and proclaimed Blok to be the major poet of his time; Bely and Sergey spoke of drafting the 'first concordat of the New Church'. Lyuba began to feel some embarrassment. The adoration was more like a monk's for the Madonna than a knight's for his lady.

Every day Blok wrote to his mother, keeping her abreast of their life in Moscow.

Sunday 11 January

At midday we were roused by Sergey's shouts. With Lyuba we went to the Sokolovs'* then to Bely's. The sunset was very red. In the evening, back to Bely's, with Balmont, Bryusov, etc. Conversation with Bryusov. Balmont read some poems, then I read some too. Bryusov recited some remarkable things, even more astonishing than his *Urbi et Orbi*. After he left, Bely and I read numerous poems. Bely is extraordinary. I read 'She is risen in the light'. Men in black frock-coats cried out and ran towards me, shouting that I was the greatest poet in the whole of Russia.

The emotional trio met at Vladimir Solovev's grave. 'The sky

*Founders of the Griff publishing house.

was terrible, purple with one green star; there was a horned moon.' There were impassioned discussions, 'serious, brilliant, marvellous conversations', and, naturally, talk of Lyuba.

Blok was now known and admired; the new journals were publishing him. He signed a contract with Griff, and his first collection of poems was announced.

Bryusov – the demon, the magician – had astonished him. For Blok, nothing could be greater or more beautiful than *Urbi et Orbi*. It was something new. No one before Bryusov had pushed Russian poetry so far towards 'modernism'. He was sonorous like Verhaeren, emancipated like Whitman, demonic like Poe, perverse like d'Annunzio, refined like Mallarmé, sensual like Baudelaire. Ten years later, all this would collapse, disperse, and all these influences, like clothes borrowed at random, would seem tiresome.

Yet at the beginning of the century, who could rival Bryusov? Balmont, drinking more and more, saw his star set rapidly. Although older than Blok, Sologub was only beginning to write. Gippius was a great poet, but was absorbed in her philosophical, theological and political ideas. Vyacheslav Ivanov was no longer in Russia, pursuing his studies abroad. And Merezhkovsky had definitely abandoned poetry in favour of novels and philosophical essays. Bryusov was on the spot and met with universal approval.

'I am writing to you at night, transported, after reading *Urbi et Orbi*. Soon I shall write poems: surely all of them will bear the mark of Bryusov,' wrote Blok to Sergey. This wonder lasted a year then, all of a sudden, it was over. 'Why are you always talking to me about Bryusov? What's done is done. A year ago, *Urbi et Orbi* pierced us all. But the wounds are beginning to heal. What he's writing now is not nearly as perfect. He is repeating himself.'

On returning to Petersburg, Blok was painfully aware of the city's coldness. He missed Moscow, where 'Bely's heart flowers'. The poems *To the Most Beautiful Lady* were finished and what Blok had vaguely foreseen in 1902, what he had feared, had happened. No one knew it yet, he hardly noticed it himself, but

> She was changing in appearance…
> I fear that you will change your form.

That mysticism, that romantic poetry attached to *Her*, on which Blok had lived for several years, was now consumed. He was at a new turning-point in his life by the time the *Verses to the Most Beautiful Lady* were issued by Griff.

One does not find, in this book of pure poetry, the 'modernism' dear to Bryusov. The 'Poor knight who never raises his helmet before his lady' (Pushkin), the amorous monk in the shadow of the church, Blok is much closer to the English and German Romantics and to Russian tales than to modern western poetry. The form is original, the melodious, flexible verse perfectly adapted to the poet's nuanced sensibility. Emphasis is often replaced by pauses – the pauses Fet and Tyutchev had so timidly tried to introduce in their poems. The rhymes are still regular; it would take a few years for Blok to make touching use of assonance.

Russian poets did not directly influence his work, with the exception of Fet, who lightly marked his first poems, and of Solovev, who had considerable influence until 1905, but none afterwards. The shock produced by reading Baudelaire, Nietzsche and Strindberg did not take effect until later. Lermontov and Tyutchev became his companions along the way until he discovered Apollon Grigoriev, whom his grandmother had known well, and who remained his favourite poet. Blok revived the memory of this poet, who died in 1864 – an unhappy, alcoholic, disowned, forgotten man, who taught him to love gypsies, guitars and the popular so-called 'cruel' romances.

The *Verses to the Most Beautiful Lady* may be read as a love story. Before his death, Blok thought of making them into an edition like Dante's *Vita Nuova*, accompanying each poem with a commentary: 'This evening I saw my Beautiful one. She looked at me. She passed nearby.'

We now know which are 'the five turnings' – the five

streets on Vasilyevsky Island – where his Lady passed, and the 'slits through which she used to look at the sun' – the tall window of the house at Boblovo. Perhaps none of that exists any longer, but the *Verses to the Most Beautiful Lady* remain as one of the most perfect works of Russian poetry.

VIII

Bely and Sergey arrived at Shakhmatovo in the summer of 1904.

Madame Kublitskaya's welcome, the attractive countryside, the old house surrounded by a garden full of flowers, the deliciously peaceful life over which Lyuba reigned, silent but utterly confident, gradually coming to delight in the adoration of her husband's friends, enchanted the young men.

The couple were there, united, still intact. Blok no longer spoke of Sophia, the figure of Wisdom, nor of 'dawns'. That luminous era was over and done with. But Bely, heavily insistent, persisted in trying to resurrect the past. Perhaps it is one solution: to be silent about the present twilight and only talk about the light of yesterday? (The Blokite 'sect' still exists. One can imagine a twenty-second-century historian, a certain Professor Lapan, writing its biography.)

They continued to ascribe prophetic meaning to Lyuba's slightest acts and gestures. Was she wearing a red dress? At once they drew manifold conclusions. Had she changed her hairstyle? They interpreted this as a 'sign'. Blok would smile. His writings reveal not a trace of jealousy. Were they all in love with his wife? There are no doubts about Sergey's feelings; he replaced the Virgin's picture in the icon's frame with a photograph of Lyuba. For Bely it was more serious: Lyuba was the only woman whom he ever really loved.

Blok and his wife spent their mornings in an annex of the old house that was covered in climbing roses. In the afternoons they went for a walk. In the evenings, on the veranda, there were passionate discussions. Lyuba kept quiet. Blok, naturally silent, let the others talk. His firm friendship with Bely was further strengthened during those weeks; their brotherliness was to be stronger than any future disagreements. According to an old custom they swapped shirts, and Bely walked about in the beautiful shirt that Lyuba had embroidered with swans. Late at night they parted. Lyuba and Blok returned to the little pink house. The guests couldn't sleep and went off for a walk, continuing their discussions.

Bely was disarmingly frank. He confessed to his own faults as simply and clearsightedly as he recognized Blok's merits. He was aware of his greatest weakness: that he never took one side in a straightforward fashion; he never knew how to say 'yes or no'. This strong, indefatigable man, a born orator, was a dialectical thinker who took refuge in compromises and half-measures, of which Blok heartily disapproved. Without wasting a moment, he let Blok know of his love for Lyuba. The atmosphere became oppressive.

What really tired Blok was the incessant game, the desire to return to the past. The air of Shakhmatovo had less of 'rose and gold', as indeed did the air over Russia in general. The war with Japan had entered into a critical phase, the first rumblings of the 1905 revolution could be heard, and Blok, with his extraordinary prescience, could feel it already. His thoughts darkened, became 'violet'.

> Linking hands
> Let us fly together into the azure!

he had written in the period of 'dawns'. But now:

> My poor wings
> Are the wings of a scarecrow.

There was no longer anyone with whom he could – or wished – to fly away.

Seventeen years later, Bely wrote in his memoir:

> We understood that Blok no longer knew his way; he was groping along, while we were constructing magnificent projects. He didn't want our projects. He knew that 'there would be night', that the 'dawns' lingered in our souls no

more. The dawn of the mind, the objective dawn – he no
longer saw them. He only saw us, we who were moving away
from the limits of the possible, who were drawing our own sky,
a sky on silk paper that the harlequin from *Balaganchik** would
easily tear.

If there was harmony no longer, friendship remained. The
summer passed. Before leaving, Bely bared his soul again,
vigorously explaining himself. Blok could only advise one
thing: that he should put an end to his feelings as quickly as
possible. Lyuba was of the same mind. Bely promised to do
so.

Bely and Sergey returned the following year, but the 'trio'
was no more. The 1905 revolution had made a deep impression on Blok; he was very serious and sombre. New themes
began to appear in his poetry and diaries. During this period
the Argonauts were all for Wundt, James, Rickert and
Solovev, arguing over the *Third Testament*, wearing themselves out in pursuit of a link between Kant and Lapan, the
twenty-second-century philosopher they'd amused themselves inventing one day. But the thread of the game was
lost. Bely was tormented by his poetic concepts, by his
impossible love for Lyuba, by his brotherly love for Blok
and, at the same time, by the discord silently undermining
their affection. Up to the last day he tried to think of Blok
as a brother and of himself as a man possessed. Lyuba grew
impatient: the feeling Bely harboured for her annoyed and
affected her. Sergey's talk, which she found pointless and
hollow, wearied her. The ardent Argonaut protested against
the incoherence of Blok's new poetic themes, and Blok did
not care for the poetry of this theologian, who wanted to
express his religious aspirations in rhyme. Understanding
and harmony were permanently destroyed. Even Madame
Kublitskaya began to dislike Sergey and no longer appreciated Bely's company.

A bitter irony pierced all Blok's phrases, the irony which
would lead him to *The Puppet Booth*. He wrote:

The Puppet Booth, a play by Blok.

> Here we are, two muddlewits —
> vapour, water, frail.
> Back-to-front the bonnet sits
> tender green and pale.

While Sergey and Bely still wanted him to 'fly together into the azure!'

So Bryusov's name recurred in their discussions: that magician, that genius was not a muddlewit! He loved sonorous verses and knew how to make them loved! Blok responded in his last, marvellous poem to the Beautiful Lady:

> You have receded into the distance, forever.
> And hallowed be your name!

And for a while this friendship dissolved: a pretext for the break-up was soon found, a misunderstanding between Madame Kublitskaya and Sergey divided the friends. Bely took Sergey's part and both returned to Moscow. There they found Bryusov again, the turbulent crowd of the magician's disciples, the literary reviews, the lectures; a life of noise and brawling. Blok and Lyuba lingered in the silence of Shakhmatovo, on the look-out for future threatening events. Lyuba asked Bely to stop writing to her; she had nothing to say to him. And, for the moment, Bely disappeared from Blok's life.

IX

On 9 January 1905 the revolution broke out. Peace with Japan had been signed – a shameful peace. The people revolted, tired of their miserable lives. Gunfire resounded through an inflamed Petersburg. In the darkness and cold of the Imperial Grenadiers' barracks – where Blok lived, in his stepfather's apartment – the soldiers waited, ready as soon as the command was given to fire on the insurgents. The easy, calm life of the preceding days now seemed like a stage-set which a breath could knock over for ever.

Blok ran down the streets, listened to what was being said, and suddenly understood that there was a life completely different from that which he had known until then, a tumultuous, hard, imposing life, the life of a whole nation – perhaps it was even real life. His mind cleared; a mass of things was revealed to him. His choice was made: to liberalism, to those who stood for a happy medium, to the echoing, empty words of the politicians touting an English-style constitution, he preferred the ancient struggle of the starving.

The tsarist regime was living out its last years. The intelligentsia were all aware of this, but already the form of the inevitable revolution had split them in two. Blok had no doubts: the people would liberate themselves, without the help of chattering politicians, without the timorous, conservative bourgeoisie, who always drew back when confronted by European opinion and the prospect of blood.

Blok talked less and less, and when he spoke, it was through clenched teeth. Seated in a deep armchair in his long, narrow study, he worked, smoked, gazed out the window. Next door to him, Lyubov was also preparing for her final exams. Her wish to be an actress surfaced for the first time during this period; she gave Blok the idea of writing for the theatre, but it was over a year before anything came to fruition.

His laughter had disappeared, his smile was grave, shadows ringed his blue-green eyes. His watchful gaze was steady. His whole person gave an impression of immobility, and those who did not care for him described him as 'carved from wood'. His rare gestures were not at all lively. He wore a loose black worsted jacket without a belt, and a white collar. His clothes had not a single crease. His hair had lost its golden lights, his cheeks their pink flush. His anguish increased; a wave of hatred rose against all the gossip, the publicity, the stupid quarrels between 'newsy' literary reviews. Solitary, he walked on the islands or along the quays full of factory noises. He liked to go to cabarets, among the people, the women who sang, got drunk and cried. In the evenings he wandered along the Vasilyevsky streets which led nowhere; behind the Smolensky cemetery – where grandfather and grandmother Beketov were buried – you could see the sea, the fiery horizon and the purple sunsets. Recollecting those years, he would write: 'We still did not know what we were waiting for, but in our hearts the needle of the seismograph was oscillating. The effect on us was of living against the background of a vast conflagration.'

He was free of Bryusov, of Moscow, of the Argonauts. Were they for the benefit of his former comrades, Sergey and even Bely, the lines –

> What in the world could be more agreeable
> Than the loss of one's best friends?

But the numbers of salons, presses, reviews increased. Blok couldn't live in the capital as though it were a desert island. He had to see people and make himself known.

Dmitry Merezhkovsky and his wife, Zinaida Gippius, were the centre of the Petersburg élite at the beginning of the century. They had a circle, just as Bryusov did, but unlike him they attracted all the thinkers rather than the creators. They were not moved by one of Rimbaud's stanzas or by an extraordinary rhyme, but by powerful and original ideas. They appealed to the 'sages'. Philosophers such as Rozanov, religious writers, novelists, poets, men of past and future revolutions, conspirators – everyone came to them because nothing left them indifferent.

The two of them formed more than a couple – a group, almost a party. He was a precursor of the great Russian literary revival, and had foreseen, as far back as 1890, the upheavals in poetic form and content.

> And we, all too precocious precursors
> Of a spring too slow in appearing.

She was the most intelligent woman of her time, slender, beautiful, elegant, with strange green eyes and magnificent red hair, dressed in furs and lace; a talented poet, novelist, critic, essayist; very biased, engaging, enjoying intellectual duels, quickly adopting every idea that appealed to her and rejecting anything that seemed frivolous.

Blok was not automatically admitted to this circle, where Merezhkovsky's essays were circulated, landmarks in the art of Russian criticism, and where Zinaida Gippius, avid for everything new, was looking for faithful adherents more than for youthful talent. Both appreciated Bryusov (who considered Gippius the greatest modern poet) in his roles as teacher and innovator. They regarded Bely with the protective and slightly irritating indulgence one has for a child or a lunatic. Bryusov and Merezhkovsky's reviews had brought Blok's first poems before the public at the same time. Who was this young man? With much curiosity, sympathy and scepticism, Gippius surveyed him through her lorgnette. His marriage to a beautiful but otherwise ordinary young woman suprised her. She had marked ideas about sexual relations; they were profoundly original and far in advance of her times. With a taste for complexity, she was disappointed by normal, conventional marriages. The young Blok was neither an opportunist nor a flatterer. He very rarely appeared, asked for nothing, kept himself to himself. If until 1918 – when they became enemies – their relations were stable as far as the Merezhkovskys were concerned, that was not at all the case with Blok. Like many others, he went through a whole gamut of varied and contradictory emotions with regard to the pair. Sometimes he detested them, blamed them for taking him over unawares, for influencing his will. Sometimes he was overcome by a desire to kiss Merezhkovsky's hands. Merezhkovsky and Gippius had their faults, even weaknesses, but they were both of Blok's stature and the three of them contributed to each other.

During the winter of 1905–1906, three encounters were to influence Blok's life: with Alexei Remizov, who became a very dear friend; with Fyodor Sologub, the poet; and with Vyacheslav Ivanov, thinker, scholar, poet, and future theoretician of Russian Symbolism.

Friend of Blok and of Bely, interested in the arts and in music, Ivanov imprinted those years with the mark of unusual thought and intelligence. After studying history and philology abroad, he had returned to Russia. Although older than Blok and Bely, he became their historical contemporary rather than Merezhkovsky's. He came to Symbolism very much by his own route: not via the French Symbolists, like Bryusov, not through Solovev, like Blok. The road he followed began in the ancient world. For him, too, Symbolism was the discovery in art of the essence of things, but in place of Bely's concept he offered one of his own. According to Ivanov, the artist does not transfigure reality when he transforms a phenomenon into an image, and an image into a symbol, thus imposing his will on the surface of things; rather, he discovers and announces the secret will of all essences in stripping away the symbols contained in reality itself. *A realibus ad realiora* – from visible truth, and, through that, to a hidden reality, even more real, of the same things – such for him was the symbolist way, which was also the ancient way of creating myths.

Stripping the symbols – that is, the signs of another reality – from the surrounding reality, the understanding conceives that which is significant. Understanding thus makes us aware of connections and meanings of that which exists not only in the realm of empirical, earthly consciousness but also of that which exists in other spheres. So genuinely symbolic art touches on the domain of religion in so far as religion is, above all, the *act* of feeling the connection which exists between everything that is and the meaning of all life.

Moving thus from Symbolism to a religious conception of art, developing and deepening his thoughts, Vyacheslav Ivanov provoked immense and ardent discussion within the Symbolist movement, its unity constantly threatened by internal disagreements – philosophical, aesthetic and religious. Nevertheless it can rightly be said that Symbolism developed in an absolutely independent manner in Russia; there, Symbolism was conscious above all of not being merely a literary school, but of having laid the foundations of a particular understanding of the world. 'Mallarmé', said Vyacheslav Ivanov, 'only wished that our thought, having completed a circle, should come down just at the point he indicated. For us, on the contrary, Symbolism is the energy which frees itself from the limits of the given world and impresses on the soul the movement of a rising spiral.'

Finally, turning towards the past, Ivanov stated an unarguable truth to be accepted by any future historian of twentieth-century Russian literature:

> The study of the work of our Symbolist school will later show to what degree Western influence was superficial, how little we reflected on what we had borrowed and what we had imitated; at bottom, how fruitless these imitations and borrowings were, and, finally, how much deeper are the roots which attach all that is authentic and viable in our poetry to our native soil.

Sologub, who was a great poet, was one of those talents whom nobody knows in their formative years. One day they burst into literature, full of wisdom and experience. Their whole oeuvre is marked by maturity. Far from the hurly-burly, factions, literary schools, superficiality, they live a mysterious, closed, secret life, apparently grumpy, disagreeable and hard to put up with. Their glory doesn't really become plain until fifty years after their death. From their very first meeting, a reciprocal sympathy and deep understanding was established between Sologub and Blok. Ivanov was a feast for the intelligence; Sologub, pure poetry.

Besides his great talent, Remizov was appreciated by Blok for the warmth of his communicative spirit, the pure and disinterested friendship he offered. Nothing effusive – Blok had a horror of that – but solid affection, always alert.

For Blok the world divided into two very uneven parts after the break with Bely: one large part to which he was absolutely indifferent; the other, restricted, chosen part he considered to be his own – it was indispensable to him and occupied all his thoughts, he had given himself to it completely and was always anxious about it. It was the same as regards places: he needed Shakhmatovo and Petersburg, sometimes he felt that they belonged to him alone. Not that he wasn't interested in people's lives or what went on in the world. But his 'own' people, his 'own' places, these were essential to him, they were his 'intimate warmth' in the sense Rozanov gives the word. Above everyone stood his wife and his mother, then a few friends to whom he was faithful unto death.

Relations with his father, who did not know how to inspire his affection or his sympathy, were correct but cold. Professor Blok took a very ironic view of the *Verses to the Most Beautiful Lady*. He became more and more pernickety and cantankerous. His second wife had left him, taking their little girl. Blok wrote to him three times a year to thank him for his allowance, given until he left university in 1906. His examinations over, Blok wrote reviews for various journals and contributed to a *History of Russian Literature*.

His mother and Lyuba shared first place in his heart. A unique harmony and intimacy bound him to his mother. Even in 1900 he could write: 'Mother and I – we often experience a feeling of melancholy with regard to all earthly things.' Two volumes of correspondence reveal their unchanging tenderness and constant anxiety. Given to fits of mental anguish, Blok's mother became more and more difficult to live with. Her jealousy, impatience and neurasthenia increased with the years, but she was part of his innermost self, she belonged to him, and his love for her never ran dry. She had wanted to see him happy, carefree, loved by women, the faithful Lyuba by his side. Yet he was too often sad, worried, irritable, and later distraught, despairing, inclined to drink. Madame Kublitskaya and Lyuba had been united in the early years of their life together. Around 1905, however, the first misunderstandings arose and rapidly widened in scope.

When he was away, Blok wrote to his mother regularly. Letters arrived from Shakhmatovo – sad, gay, serious, playful. He sent her the first violet and gave her news of life in the fields.

'They've purchased a bull. The boar is an adorable creature: he cost twenty-one roubles. I'm not writing. All my thoughts are about the geese, the turkeys and the piglets. They say that the two geese are "brothers". That's why they don't lay.'

But more often he spoke of his torments, of his inner life.

'My nerves are jangled. I want to rest. I will try not to begin arguing again [with his stepfather]… anyway I won't be doing much talking.' He didn't hide any thoughts, knowing that she would always understand him.

It would be good to invent something other than language for conversations. Words are beginning to wear out. People talk too much.

I'm becoming wild and many words just don't reach me.

When I get out of Petersburg into the fields, I feel better than I feel anywhere else.

Dostoevsky comes back to life in every corner of the town. We went down to where the Fontanka comes out, after the Kalinkin Bridge. We sat down on a little boat with holes. Kids were playing; a ragged painter was painting a landscape. In the distance, the cruisers' sirens were hooting...

When he left the grenadier barracks to settle with Lyuba in their own apartment, he wrote to his mother setting out plainly the nature of their relationship:

Mama, I'm at home and I want to write to you because when we see each other we don't talk, we only argue. I am very tense these days, and I want to be even more so. Contact with people doesn't tire me, it revives my personality which I like more and more. I find myself in a state of violent exaltation which prevents my noticing what is going on around me. And at such moments you look at me inquiringly. I would like you to know that at every moment of my life whatsoever I love you. I also love Franz and aunt. Lyuba loves you too, she often tells me so. I want these truths to be clear, always, otherwise a lot of silly things will spoil our life. Furthermore, I feel that relations, the other members of the family, all acquaintances are odious. They cannot know and must know who I am. They are as far from me as the policemen who watch passers-by...

Autumn 1906: a turning-point. The end of university. Blok is a well-known, loved, celebrated poet. He has his own flat where he receives his intimates; he goes into 'the world'. In Ivanov's 'Tower', at Sologub's Sundays, he is feted and acclaimed. He is welcome at the Merezhkovskys, he has an aura of fame and even of fashion.

But his poems are bitterly ironic, infinitely despairing. On his solitary rambles he stops off at low dives, not as spectator but as companion and accomplice of the drunks and the girls.

X

> From the troika-driver to the greatest poet
> All of us, singing sadly...

said Pushkin. And Gogol in turn remarked: 'There is something terrible in the destiny of Russian poets.'

In Russia, the nineteenth century was that of tragic destinies; the twentieth, that of suicides and premature deaths. Blok used to say that the last serene face among European poets was Schiller's. Among Russian poets, you couldn't find a serene face. The previous century had been cruel to them. Pushkin at thirty-seven, Lermontov at twenty-seven, met their deaths in duels which might have been avoided. Ryleyev was hanged. Sometime before his death, Fet, aged seventy-seven, wanted to slash his stomach. Apollon Grigoriev, the talented Fofanov, died of misery and alcoholism. Tyutchev's life was a long succession of sufferings, and it was only after his death that it was known what torments devoured Annensky. Not to mention frustrated destinies, because Russia is *par excellence* the land of frustrated destinies!

Blok's drunkenness was not at all like Grigoriev's. In 1860, Grigoriev drank to forget his poverty, the cramped life of minor nobility come down in the world in a dreadful provincial hole, his wife worn out by sorrows and cares, his barefoot children, the constant threat of debtors' prison and the lack of clean shirts which prevented his going out. Dead drunk, he no longer recognized anyone, forgot everything.

Blok never lost his lucidity. It wasn't wine but despair that was destroying him. 'Life took this shape': the liking for fleeting encounters, the feverish search for something he lacked, which he wanted to find by whatever means, gypsy songs, the waste of dreary years, the desire to forget the minor betrayals by Bely, and Lyuba, advancing into the unknown of her career as an artist.

In his poems, in his letters, his articles, his diaries, in all of Blok's work and even in successive photographs, can be seen the awful, implacable crescendo of infinite anguish, as though the twenty-four years of his life as a man had been nothing but perpetual heartbreak.

His laughter disappeared, and then his smile. Conversation became rarer and, soon, so did words. His complexion altered from pink to yellow and then to muddy. The golden hair became grey and thinner. In his poetry the 'Dawns' were extinguished first, and then the 'sunsets', leaving mist, snowstorms, whirlwinds... The air faded from purple to violet, then to grey, then black. And the music which he had heard inside himself since childhood, and which was the breath of the universe to him, became more and more distant, and died...

Blok was twenty-six. He finished his collection of poems, *Joy Unhoped-for*. What meagre, feeble joy, laced with bitter irony! Not only the Argonauts – the group had broken up – but all those who thought of Blok as 'the poet of the Lady', the 'troubadour of Beauty', were disappointed. You might like these poems less than Blok's youthful work, and find them less perfect, but what Blok himself said about them is absolutely true: if they hadn't been written, those of his third period – his most beautiful, his greatest – wouldn't have come into existence.

The miserable landscapes of Shakhmatovo (so there were not only rosy Dawns) and the gloomy crossroads of Petersburg form a poignant backdrop to these poems. Blok now knew the intoxication of wine. 'She' had gone forever. Little devils 'in green caps, worn askew' capered round him. The rhymes became less studied, the rhythm more wayward and, in the verdigris mirrors of a restaurant, its walls naively painted with boats (was it on the islands, or on the houseboat they loved to visit?), he discovered a new woman, the Stranger – this one accessible – whom the whole world could see, touch, admire, love.

The gypsy violins accompanied them to the door. The sleigh was waiting, with its cosy bearskin. Slender, supple, black-haired, with gleaming teeth and green almond-shaped eyes, covering her face with her muff, making her warm laugh ring out through the freezing night, she disappeared with him into the wind and snow. The air was scented with champagne and her perfume. The foaming horse skimmed along by the Neva. False vows, true kisses, tears of happiness – it was all there!

> I spent a year of folly
> In the train of a lady in black.

She was Natalya Volokhova, an actress in Meyerhold's theatre. For more than a year she ruled over him. His violent passion for her, the intoxication he knew beside her, produced a mixture of joy, anguish, exaltation and fulfilment. It was she who inspired the poems of the *Snow Mask* and *Faina*. The form changed, new rhythms and unusual rhymes appeared.

Throughout this year Blok was very interested in the theatre, especially in Volokhova's. This infatuation, far from separating him from Lyuba, drew them closer; more than ever, she wanted to be an actress. Meyerhold, one of the greatest directors,* was at that point the head of a young company. He brought his friends to Blok's; everyone was thrilled by the poet and they asked him to write something for them. The company was full of ideas. The old theatre of manners had gone, and with it the old ways of life. It was necessary to create not only a new theatre but new ways of living, sweeping away convention and throwing off restraint, rejecting duties and obligations, all of the hallowed life, making each day either a feast or a torment! Meyerhold was the driving force of the company; Vera Kommissarzhevskaya – the 'Russian Duse' – the actor-manager. All these young people, passionate about the

---

*Arrested in 1939, he was shot in Moscow on 2 February 1940.

theatre and liberty, had ideas and clearly defined aims which they struggled hard to realize, ready to pay for their triumphs with their lives. Blok, with his hatred of the conventional and solidly established, relaxed in this circle. Lyuba had obtained a part and, with some of the company, was playing in the provinces. Meyerhold wanted Blok to write something in response to their ideas. Blok wrote *The Puppet Booth*.

A little theatre with tightrope walkers, a fairground stall, where a sad Pierrot waits for his Columbine, whom the Harlequin will take from him. The Beautiful Lady is cardboard, the sky – where the happy lovers fly away – is tissue paper. Liquid flows from the wound of the poor abandoned lover, and the 'mystics' who jabber their 'theories' in chorus remain open-mouthed, become quite flat and disappear, while the author, pestered from right and left, doesn't know what to dream up to explain to the audience what has just happened.

Those who understood the poems of his second period did not regard *The Puppet Booth* as a farce but as an extremely serious and painful stage in Blok's oeuvre. His illusions ripped apart, he was wounded by the agonizing emptiness.

The Argonauts were furious, rightly recognizing themselves in the gossiping 'mystics'. Bely was beside himself; he could accept their former jokes about Lapan and so forth, but that Blok should ridicule the Lady (just cardboard) and the sky (just tissue) and the mystics (two-dimensional) was unbearable to the adorer of the Universal Soul and the lover of Lyuba.

1906–7: an endless, complicated series of quarrels and reconciliations between Blok and Bely. Their meetings – almost always at Bely's request – were painful. Blok remained in perfect control of himself – cold, polite, never wounding, saying charming things in his slightly superior tone. Bely, nervous, breathless, sometimes overflowing with affection, sometimes heavy with hatred, challenged him to a duel, then demanded an explanation in order to forgive or to be forgiven. He felt totally extraneous to Blok's life, and

53

had moments of self-loathing in imposing himself on Blok, who bore with him out of pity for his unrealized genius, though he was also disarmed by Bely's sincerity when he accused himself of all his faults and recognized his wrongs, never speaking of his own attributes and merits, although they were many.

Blok endured but did not seek these encounters. One day Bely arranged to meet him in a restaurant. Blok arrived, accompanied by Lyuba. Bely was mad with joy: everything was still possible. But a few days later, everything was spoiled again. Right in the middle of Nevsky Prospekt, Blok — absorbed in his thoughts, haughty and unapproachable — passed him by. For Bely this had 'the effect of a blow'.

Another time they read poetry all night long, in perfect harmony. Sergey and the Argonauts were forgotten, banished for once and for all. Bely swore to settle down for good in Petersburg. But Blok's poem *The Night Violet* destroyed all that. 'No, it won't do! Sergey is clearly right — Blok renounces everything, is nothing but a twirling butterfly, brushing every subject, not even understanding what he's doing.'

'You don't fool me!' Bely repeated, enraged, listening to Blok's latest poems.

And then there was his deception in *The Puppet Booth*, almost a farce. 'There was a hole where his spirit used to be,' wrote Bely in his memoirs. He wanted to flee Moscow for good. Lyuba, of whom he had demanded explanations, was most amused by his tragic air, his sadness and his disappointment. He would never make up his mind to leave. He had the mad idea of fighting Blok. In Moscow, in Bryusov's journals, he violently attacked the new Blok, who went on smiling, unassailable. Bely recounts in his frank memoirs his attempts to separate Lyuba from her husband, by any means. But Lyuba was already very distant from it all; it could no longer touch her. A desire had awakened in her to live her own life, to be a real woman and not a symbol.

'I was close to him,' writes Bely, 'and did not understand

him. I did everything to make things worse for him; I rubbed salt in his wounds.'

Blok never raised his voice; Bely was under the impression that he condescended to speak to him, which made Bely mad.

They separated; they met again. Bely was struck by the alteration in Blok's features. A deep, vertical crease ran down his forehead. His voice had become harsh. He was drinking. Bely angrily attacked: 'You are nothing but petit-bourgeois!' To which Lyuba replied: 'You've become a megalomaniac!' Bely no longer went out without a revolver and black eye-mask in his pocket. People warned Blok that he was spoiling for a duel, but Blok replied, 'I think he's just very tired.'

Bely went to Munich and stayed there a year. When he returned to Moscow, everybody was talking about Blok, and his scathing, vicious criticism had no effect. He mobilized the remainder of the Argonauts and engineered Bryusov's opposition to Blok, as his continually increasing fame threatened the Master's. At the same time, he listened avidly to all the gossip about Blok and about Lyuba. Three painful echoes reached his ears: Blok was drinking, Blok was passionately in love with Natalya Volokhova, and Blok was continuing to write pieces for the theatre in the style of *The Puppet Booth*. Bely published a collection of poems: *Ashes*.

He had done everything to provoke a stunning and final break-up, but neither his intrigues nor his attacks, nor even the unusually impertinent letter he sent on his return from Munich, achieved his aim. And this time it was Blok who called him. A new explanation: Blok held Sergey Solovev responsible for all the quarrels, and Bely blamed Lyuba. Blok proposed to make peace, and not to involve anyone else in their friendship; to seal their reconciliation the two went off to Kiev to give a lecture. They returned to Petersburg, happy; Bely feared meeting Lyuba but everything passed off well; he received a simple and affectionate welcome. Yet something had certainly changed. Lyuba was no longer the same: very confident, worldly, popular, she spoke happily of her successes. Like Blok she was leading her own life, independent and individual. The evenings lacked the intimate charm of the old days, when Bely used to linger far into the night in Blok's study or in the dining-room with Lyuba; they used to read, argue, stay silent, and even the silences were treasured. Now Blok, distant and often drunk, would disappear, sometimes for several days. Lyuba, very busy, acted and received her friends. A crack had appeared in their life together, a coldness which froze Bely. One day Lyuba swore that she had lived through terrible things that had almost destroyed her. And Blok said bitterly that he had 'crossed the Rubicon' and that there was no way back. The peace and harmony so much admired by Bely in 1904 were far away. Madame Kublitskaya, whose relationship with Lyuba was deteriorating, rarely came round. The house was full of people with whom Bely had nothing in common. Lyuba and Volokhova, despising the old conventions, got on tremendously well and were friends, which seemed extraordinary and shocked the 'provincial Muscovite'. Volokhova's power over Blok was limitless; second-rate, insignificant people took the place of old friends. People said that Lyuba and Blok had replaced their life with a theatre. But 'there was no going back'.

Bely couldn't take it any more; he suffered miserably in this entourage which he couldn't stand. Lyuba grew more and more distant. Despairing, he returned to Moscow and for several years all contact between him and Blok would cease; they wouldn't even write to each other. Bely's memories were of Blok's new face: no longer that of their youth, when he resembled Gerhardt Hauptmann, but a heavier, wearier face, which reminded Bely of Oscar Wilde's.

XI

Mama, life weighs on me more and more. There is such cold all around me. A space is forming, as if all the world had left me, as though no one loved me. I'm living on a desolate island, cold and empty. Good-hearted people don't come here any more. On this island there are three of us, oddly connected. The two of them have restless souls, very different and yet very much alike. They, too, are terribly cold.

But the 'year of folly' passed. Without even saying goodbye, Volokhova and Blok parted.

'Perhaps it is not really you after all?' he wrote; and again, 'I don't know any more, I have forgotten you.'

An end to the evenings as a trio; now he was alone. Lyuba, on tour, happy in her work and her success, remained affectionate towards Volokhova. Bewildered, disheartened, Blok stayed behind as if after a shipwreck, without the strength to rally. 'I drink a lot, I live in a horrible fashion, and as always not like the rest of the world.'

'Mama, living is painful for me. Solitude leads me into dives; I wander round and I drink. I'm going to the bad, my life is ruined. But which of us doesn't have a ruined life?'

Some friends gathered around him, men without much talent but with whom it was pleasant enough to pass an evening drinking, chatting, walking aimlessly. Evgeny Ivanov, unfailing in his devotion, and Pyast, a visionary in love with Strindberg, were the most faithful. In his despair and fear of solitude, Blok accepted their company.

'Why not drink, since life has taken this turn?'

'Mama, this week has been so stupid: black and tormented. I would willingly sell my life, but for pure gold, not to keep a home.'

Nevertheless, Lyuba's return made him happy. Her grace,

her charming gestures, her smiling face calmed him down. She restored order to his life: he liked seeing the house clean again, the curtains fresh, his books nicely arranged. But already another tour called her away; once Lyuba left, Blok again became taciturn, sad, with 'a stony smile'. Even Shakhmatovo held no attraction for him: he was bored by its woods and plains, and above all he missed terribly those fleeting, chance encounters. Natalya Volokhova, *The Stranger,** the woman who became a star, the passer-by with her black train who changed into a comet, had disappeared from his life. But others came, and came without stopping.

> She is called Marta; she has two long plaits. I knew how to make a prostitute into a tender, passionate woman in three hours. Everything about her is a mystery. Her simple soul becomes a harp from which I can draw any note. Real passion is so rare, yet without passion there can't be anything except physical desire. Sometimes passion comes like a storm. Sometimes in a cloud of sadness. Sometimes as a liberation.
>
> [*Diaries*]

> Mama, I spent the night with a very beautiful woman. After many adventures I found myself with her at four o'clock in the morning, in a hotel. I got back to the house around nine.

A few months before his death, Blok declared that there had been nearly three hundred such encounters. A few of these women live on in his poetry; the others have disappeared without trace.

Then boredom set in, that inheritance from the previous century which, before the other war, existed in Russia in a new form. It was no longer the dreary torpor in which the provinces foundered in the nineteenth century – minds numbed, stomachs too full – lost in the midst of the track-less steppes, far from the large towns. Nor the boredom of Chekhov's heroes! It was a greenhouse atmosphere, in which thousands lived, in a sterile, dangerous, amoral isolation, without any contact with the great mass of uneducat-

*A little play by Blok, with the same title as the famous poem.

ed, poverty-stricken people. Were they exhausted and crippled by having sprouted too soon, these greenhouse specimens? Or had the people stagnated for five hundred years? The history of Russia might be the evolution of boredom, transformed over centuries in its vast spaces, under the too-grey sky, into passivity, heavy cruelty and laziness. Blok, like so many others, was overtaken by this boredom and often, stretched out on his bed for hours on end, despairingly contemplated the flies circling the lamp – the eternal symbol of Russian *ennui*.

The 1905 revolution played a large part in forming Blok by putting him in direct touch with life, by revealing to him a life other than that of ideas, philosophies and religions. Symbolism, Bely's fiery speeches, Vyacheslav Ivanov's 'too-precious' articles were certainly important, indeed very valuable, but they were all *maudit*. Something else was needed in Russia. Did one have the right to be interested in Diaghilev's ballets, to be gripped by Corbière's poems as translated by Bryusov, to sing of the beauty of Greek heroes when the storm was so close? All that was so enticing, and no one wanted to know anything. Blok wasn't asking the Russian élite to act immediately, to renounce Beauty, which he himself couldn't live without adoring. Unlike Nekrasov, he didn't require his friends to become 'citizens'. It was simply that once he'd understood this 'curse of the abstract' which weighed on Russian intellectuals, he stopped in the middle of the street and said to them: 'Cover your faces! Cover your heads with ashes! The time is at hand.'

In her memoirs, Madame Gippius said that Blok had something 'defenceless' about him. What defence was possible for someone who had *understood*? Bely and the others often spoke about his pride, the way he held his head high, his 'stony smile', his habit of not opening his mouth even when reading out his poems. He was above all proud of *knowing*, of being prepared for the catastrophe for which there was no cure.

The 1905 revolution profoundly enriched him and made

him want to set down his thoughts in the form of articles. From 1907 to 1918, Blok wrote a remarkable series of articles, 'Russia and the Intelligentsia'.

All these men from the élite, cultivated, wicked, growing old over their discussions about Christ, with their wives and sisters-in-law dressed in the latest fashion, all these philosophers and priests in shining contentment, knowing that beyond their doors are the 'poor in spirit', who need not words but action! A poor little priest in a shabby robe calls on Jesus: all the world gazes and finds that indecent. An honest socialist with a wrinkled forehead angrily poses a dozen questions. A bald head, reeking of incense, shies away: it's impossible to answer you, you're asking too much at once! Such meetings have become fashionable and are very pleasant for patronesses and professors' wives.

Meanwhile the wind blows. The girls on the pavement are cold. People are hungry. They are judged; they are hanged. This is the 'reaction'. It is difficult, it is hateful, it is terrible to live in Russia. I wish that the too-solid flesh of these chatterers would melt as they speak. Nobody needs them, apart from a few refined souls! They are no good to Russia…

If the will to die is increasingly frequent among the Russian intelligentsia, the people have always had the will to live. That is why even the unbelievers go to them, looking for the life-force in them. They are led by an instinct for self-preservation. They throw themselves on the people only to meet with silence, mocking smiles, pity, disdain. It is a line that cannot be crossed – or perhaps something even more terrible and more unexpected.

Gogol and other Russian writers liked to think of Russia as the embodiment of sleep and silence. But this sleep is coming to an end; the silence is being replaced by a distant, growing rumble which has nothing in common with the noise of our great cities.

Gogol pictured Russia as a flying troika: 'Russia, where are you flying to? Answer! She gives no answer. The bells fill the air with their mysterious sound… ' [*Dead Souls*]

This rumbling which grows ever louder, which we hear more clearly every year, is it perhaps that 'mysterious sound'? And what if the troika, tearing the air as it thunders along, creating a blast, what if it hurls itself at us? Even as we cast ourselves at the feet of the people, we are casting ourselves under the furious troika, to certain death. Why do we know two sensations so well: absolute joy and absolute despair? Soon there will be no others! Perhaps because around us it is already dark. In the darkness we feel we are alone, we no longer sense other people. We seem to have the impression that, as in a nightmare, looming above is the shaggy chest of the centre horse, and that his heavy hooves are about to crush us. [1908]

It seems that my contemporaries have found a bomb beside them. Each reacts according to character. Some try to defuse it. Others, terrified and frozen, gaze at it: is it going to explode? Still others act as though nothing is out of the ordinary, as though this round gadget is merely an orange, as though in a good farce. And others, lastly, take flight, trying not to attract any criticism of their behaviour…

In each of us, whether we will or no, there is this feeling of unease, of anguish, of breaking, of calamity. No one can deny it, yet there is protest when the subject is raised. If you say that in every family there is something not quite right, you will find someone who'll swear that he's lived peacefully with his wife and children for twenty-five years. If you say that science can do nothing about the dreadful earthquakes in southern Italy, some scientist will tell you that in three thousand years nature will be tamed once and for all.   [1908]

The most sensitive, the most lively children of our century have been attacked by an illness unknown to doctors. This illness is a kind of mental illness. It is called 'irony'. It is manifested in fits of exhausting laughter, which begin with a provoking, mocking smile and end up in violent blasphemy. One would like to laugh along with these 'irony patients', but one can't believe in them… Don't listen to our laugh! Listen to the pain behind the laughter. Do not believe in any of us. Believe in what is beyond us.   [1908]

61

One cannot foresee everything, or guess everything. Blood and fire may begin to talk when people least expect it. Russia, having emerged from one revolution, is staring into the eyes of another, which will come, and which may be even more terrible. [1913]

These were Blok's thoughts in the years following the first revolution. For those who lived in Moscow as for those who lived in Petersburg, one thing was undeniable: Blok was no longer the Lady's troubadour; he was a man of contemporary Russia, with a heavy conscience, full of incurable anguish; he was looking at the future with clear eyes. He was becoming greater than his school, greater than his masters; he was not afraid of words, he was not ashamed of tears.

XII

The three parts of Blok's first book made a perfectly harmonious whole. This was not so with the second book, written between 1904 and 1908. There we find the cycle *The Bubbles of the Earth* which so shocked Bely; *The City*, reflecting Blok's walks round the squalid areas of Petersburg's suburbs; the *Free Thoughts*, unrhymed, in decasyllabic lines; numerous poems dedicated to Volokhova (*The Snow Mask, Faina*), and lastly, *Various Poems*. It is these, above all, which show the path Blok trod during those years.

The world had never possessed great density for Blok; he saw through it to a mass of grander, deeper, more significant and essential things. After the revolution, after his own crisis, at the beginning of the first punishing year (1908), Blok's thoughts took a new turn. He became aware of the fragility of everything around him. The frame began to show through the thick stone walls, the skeleton became discernible beneath the warm, pink flesh. The scenery was going to collapse, this life would vanish, the whole country might founder! This notion settled on him and took hold. He wanted to fight such forebodings. But Dostoevsky had said that Petersburg would melt away one day. And if the whole of Russia should melt away too? If sun and wind should dispel all the mist only to reveal thousands of kilometres of silence, swamp, forests – limitless wilderness? Like its artificial capital, the whole of Russia, a mere phantom, would vanish. The capital was handsome, though, and solidly supported on granite. But wasn't Rome also strongly defended? As Italy had replaced the Roman Empire, so something would exist instead of Russia. It might be very beautiful, and some tourists would like it even more than the ancient monuments. But it wouldn't be the same. Rome had perished and Russia, like Rome, would perish. 'Russia, like Rome, is drunk on you', wrote Blok in his poem to Cleopatra.

And a whole era would vanish along with Petersburg, the great era of Russian poetry that began with Pushkin. Peter the Great's two gifts would meet the same end, on the same day.

In *The Night Violet*, Blok spoke of the city's transparent setting for the first time. Time was away, everything had stopped, everything was asleep. On the banks of the Neva people from a thousand years ago, sunk in a deep torpor, dreamed as they gazed at the sea. Thus for perhaps two thousand years they would stare in front of them, and the ageless daughter of the king, himself grandson of the Vikings, would spin day and night, century after century. For the first time, Blok expressed life's fragility, the precariousness of the setting which had seemed indestructible until then. And we sense that if all this must disappear one day, then the glorious period of which Blok is the last representative will also disappear.

Everything was going to crumble. Blok had no doubt of that, and sounded the knell in his poems, his articles, his diaries. But people refused to believe it; they didn't want to hear what he was saying. Some deepened their theories of Symbolism, others became interested in politics or lost themselves in the subtleties of religious argument. The twenty-year-olds made their noisy literary entrances, deliberately reacting against the ideas of Bely and Ivanov. Perhaps only Remizov and Sologub understood Blok, but they were both too absorbed in their own thoughts and writing.

As prophet of the revolution, Blok attracted no attention from left-wing parties who, with their outmoded tastes and deafness towards new art forms, only saw him as a sophisticate, decadent and useless. The liberal wing, whom Blok couldn't stand and who represented to him everything bourgeois, rightly regarded him as an enemy, scolded him for predicting an appalling future and preventing people from sleeping with his funereal knell.

Blok aligned himself with everything that must perish; he observed in himself the slide towards destruction. His anguish was the world's; the next disaster would be the end of everything he loved, the end of the Petersburg era, the end of peaceful Shakmatovo, the end of a society, of a set of ideas which would be destroyed by the same fatal, implacable force which was destroying his own hearth.

> Ah, if you only knew, children,
> The cold and shadows of the days to come!*

Not a hint of fear, only desperation. It wasn't Slavic fatalism that prevented Blok reacting. It was his amazing lucidity: 'We cannot hide it, we have the right to declare it; we can permit ourselves to be pessimists through and through.'

The year 1908 was the first of the punishing years. From one of his notebooks for November 1908 come the following excerpts, which give a glimpse of Blok's state of mind:

> Everything is calm. Suddenly, from the room next door – his voice:
> – A-a-ah!
> – What is it?
> He runs in, holding his head.

> – How strange it all is. I was dreaming. The curtain went up. Syphilitics were painfully climbing the mountain. And all of a sudden, I was one of them. Save me!
> – The child mustn't hear you!

> Nightmares. Impossible to open my mouth.

> They carry a man wounded by a brick.
> – Yes, my God, yes, my God, it doesn't matter, I'll get better; it was an accident.
> – It wasn't an accident.

> But I am so handsome, so strong, why this?

> For me the most important thing is that they should understand what I call my *Memento mori* – terrible and true.

---

*He was not the only one to have thought so. The philosopher Konstantin Leontiev, born in 1831, said that 'Russia's thousand-year-old civilization had reached its end' and that 'its future existence was dubious'. Leontiev arrived at this conclusion after a long chain of historical reasons. Blok felt it and lived it.

XIII

Besides several poems in Blok's second volume reflecting his love for Volokhova, there is a play, *The Song of Fate*, also clearly inspired by his passion. This failed play, which has never been performed, is undoubtedly the worst thing Blok ever wrote. While strongly influenced by *Peer Gynt* and the drama of Hauptmann and Maeterlinck, its curiosity value lies in its autobiographical element, and its interest in the mentality of the hero who, happy – too happy – at his wife's side, goes off and, far from his tranquil home, encounters emotional storms.

'God! I can't go on any longer. I am too happy at home. Give me the strength to tear myself away and see what the world is like. I only want to keep my burning, youthful soul and my conscience alive. Lord, I ask no more of you this pure spring evening, when my thoughts are so clear and calm.

'Is there a man alive who could bear such calm? A living man is torn. He looks around and sees nothing but tears. He looks into the distance and is drawn to the distance.'

And the hero adds, 'I don't need a hearth, calmness; I need the whole world with its singing wind.'

With *The Snow Mask*, *Faina* and *Various Poems*, Blok's talent came of age. Nothing juvenile remained. The form is very personal, the choice of words is severe. There is not a trace of romanticism: simple words, everyday words, strong and precise, lead him from *The City* to *The Twelve*. There is less of the countryside: walls, stones, courtyards. He controls his rhythms with extraordinary virtuosity, giving his poetry considerable charm and originality. The gypsy romance appears with its violins, its guitars, drink and dance. These poems have a past and suggest a future, and from this future a new theme emerges: death.

These collections brought him glory. He was acclaimed in Petersburg, in Moscow, in Kiev. Newspapers and journals published his articles. At Sologub's, at the Merezhkovskys', in Ivanov's 'Tower', he was the long-awaited, most feted guest. His translation of Grillparzer's *Die Ahnfrau* was performed in Petersburg.

Lyuba gave birth to a child, who died after ten days. She returned to Blok. Their life could now be sorted out: she would stay at his side, look after him, and go with him to Italy in the summer. In his diaries he speaks of the joy he felt in her presence; he loved her charming face, her carefree ways, her childishness. He records with pleasure that she grows lovelier and younger in Venice. He needs her; she is the Only One.

'I'm afraid of death, I'm afraid of life. The past is the dearest thing to me. Lyuba is the sacred in my soul. She helps me. How? I don't know. Perhaps because she has captured me entirely...'

They visited the Accademia, the Doges' Palace. Blok, sensitive to Renaissance art, admired the annunciations above all. Strolling through the rooms, it seemed to him that he sometimes recaptured the atmosphere of the period of the Beautiful Lady.

'Come back, come back,' he said, as though returning to his past. 'Come back at the end of our trials. To you we address our prayers in the midst of all the fears and all the passions to come. Again I await you, your slave, who has betrayed you but returned. Leave me my poignant memories. Do not soften my anguish, do not shorten my torments. Let me see your light. Come back!'

At the same time he was writing an erotic poem:

> To be with the Virgin, in the night,
> Rocking on the waves of the sea...

These were only passing inspirations. Something else touched him more deeply in the course of this Italian trip: Russia. For the first time he saw his country from the outside, from a distance, and it made a terrible impression.

He had already written to his mother, several days before leaving:

> I came home last night, shattered, after the *Three Sisters*. It is a fragment of great Russian art which, by luck or miracle, remains unspoilt; it is a fragment of my country – dirty, limited, bloody – which, thank God, I'm leaving tomorrow.
>
> We are all unhappy. Our homeland prepares the ground for our anger and quarrels. Each of us lives behind the Great Wall of China, in mutual distrust. Our only real enemies – the government, the priests, vodka, the crown, the police – hide their faces and set us against one another. I shall endeavour to forget all Russian 'politics', all our incompetence, all this mess, to become a man and not a machine breathing hatred. One must choose: either not to live here... to spit once and for all in the drunken face of Holy Russia, or to isolate oneself entirely, to take shelter from the humiliations of political life as from social life.

In Venice this feeling and these ideas were reinforced.

> My poor Russia, with her ridiculous government, her infantile intelligentsia! I would deeply despise her myself, if I were not Russian... Each of us has the right, for a while, to stop his ears, to forget things Russian, in order to know his second homeland, Europe.
>
> The only place I can live in is Russia, but terrible things are going on there, as nowhere else. Where to go? When you arrive, they rob you, and in the interior, they hang you. And censorship will filch everything I'll write...

Europe, however, offered him no better escape than Russia:

> More than ever I see that I can never accept this life, and until my death I shall never be able to submit to it. The shameful ruling order inspires me with disgust, and nothing but disgust. One can change nothing; no revolution will change anything. Men are just swine. I love only art, children and death. For me, Russia will only ever be of sentimental value. In truth she doesn't exist, has never existed, will never be.

From the same vantage point, he judged his life. Weary and bored, he thought of all the literary and political agitation in Petersburg. To be free! To be free – that is, to have no need of earning a living by writing. 'It must all be changed before it is too late. Find something else, some way of not having to earn money by the pen. One has to live, after all!'

My art, my dear art, which my friends insistently demand of me, will remain inside me, secretly, without... without Chulkov, without 'those young ladies', without journals, without lectures, without charity *soirées*, without all those *artistes* and their hysterical laughter.

I should like to think a lot, live tranquilly, see very few people, work, study. Will that be impossible? Everything political must be brushed aside. Then I might be able to create something again... And Lyuba would help me.

One can exist without Bugayev and Solovev.

Florence, Siena... For the moment these are only luminous patches. Soon they will be poems, the *Italian Verses* of his third volume, the most classical of his works.

He left Milan and returned via Bad Neuheim. Twelve years had gone by since his first visit. Memories of his first love – its sweetness and charm – woke in him. He jotted down in his notebook: 'My first love, if I'm not fooling myself, was followed by a profound disgust for the act. (Impossible to unite with a woman who is too beautiful; one must love those less beautiful.)'

He returned to Russia with Lyuba. It was summer, Shakhmatovo was waiting. But Blok was no longer content there. Why? What had happened? He didn't know. He was bored in the place that had been so dear to him, he was bored between his wife and his mother who tried hard to make him happy. He loved Lyuba. She was the only woman he had truly loved; he loved her and would love her all his life. But to see no one but her in this monotonous country-side became unbearable. Moreover, he wanted to be alone.

His mother was having epileptic fits; she would have to

be sent to a sanatorium. The farmer was giving them nothing but problems; he would have to be sent back. But there was no money, and everything dragged on.

In Petersburg, too, life dragged. Autumn came in very sadly, despite the renewed fame that the *Italian Verses* brought him. He wrote various articles, not only in the avant-garde journals but also in the popular press. He wanted to put on his *Song of Fate*; that, too, dragged on!

> For three weeks I've not left the house. It is very painful for me. The only consoling thing is this appalling terror that reigns everywhere. All Russians are on the road to ruin, taking the country with them. The 'solid order' is established, that's plain. The feet and fists of the Russians are attached separately to each person, but also each to each. Every movement harms one's neighbour, bound like me. These are the conditions of individual and social life! Everywhere, throughout Russia, it's the same. Everywhere a stink, dirt, asphyxiation. And it was always thus: this country has neither history nor art nor anything on which a life could be based. And that is why life has no point.

Already the second punishing year was on its way. Blok was called to Warsaw: his father had just died.

XIV

Retribution – Blok's great poem, unfortunately never finished – was conceived in Warsaw in the days following the funeral rites for Professor Blok. The epigraph is from Ibsen: 'Adolescence, it's retribution'. The work was born out of the poet's posthumous love for the father who, throughout his life, had been a complete stranger to him.

When Blok began to write *Retribution*, in 1910, his poetic genius was at its height. The prologue and the first chapter are perfect works of art. The second chapter is unfinished, the third scarcely broached. Russian poetry rarely attains this prophetic grandeur. This is the gist of the preface to the poem, written in 1919.

> Because this poem will never be finished, I should like to recount how it came about and the reasons for its existence. It is not pointless, for oneself and for others, to recall the birth of one's work. We, the happiest of the unhappy children of our century, are obliged to preserve our whole lives in our memories. For us each year has a different colour and remains, alas! unforgettable. Each date is written in blood. We can forget nothing: our lives are written in our faces.
>
> *Retribution*, conceived in 1910, was mainly written in 1911. What was happening in those years?
>
> In 1910, Vera Kommissarzhevskaya died, Vrubel died,* and Tolstoy. The lyrical note in the theatre disappeared with Kommissarzhevskaya. A vast world died with Vrubel, his own and all the researches that led him to madness. Tenderness and human wisdom went with Tolstoy.
>
> 1910 was also the year of crisis for Symbolism. The year of new poetic schools, enemies of Symbolism and of each other:

---

*Mikhail Vrubel (1856–1910), a painter whom Blok had never met but who fascinated him. Blok was asked to speak at his graveside. – Trs.

Acmeism, Ego-futurism, the first signs of Futurism.

Winter 1911 for me was full of deep unease and of vigorous effort. I remember long discussions from which one thing emerged: art, life and politics are inseparable and at the same time opposed to one another. Thought, woken by events, knocked at these three doors; it could no longer content itself with the artificial agreement and apparent harmony which ruled in the mystical twilight at the beginning of the century, and in the years immediately after the first revolution, bringing the intoxication of a false mysticism.

The vigorous current triumphed. It demanded harmony between contradictory elements. Then one heard the cruel voice of Strindberg – a year before his death. Already one could smell burning, iron and blood. In 1911, Milyukov gave a lecture entitled 'The Armed Peace and Armaments Reduction'. A Moscow journal published an article on 'The Approach of War'. In Kiev, Andrey Yushchinsky was killed and people talked of Christian blood being used in Jewish rituals. That summer it was extraordinarily hot: the grass was scorched. Great strikes began in London and, in the Mediterranean, the Agadir incident ignited.

On top of all that, for me, was the craze for circus wrestling; thousands of spectators began to take an interest in wrestling. And also the beginning of aviation, the first acrobatic flights and the deaths of aviators. Finally, in the autumn, Stolypin was killed in Kiev, and power slid from semi-noble, semi-bureaucratic hands into the hands of the Tsarist police.

All these facts, for me, had a musical direction, a musical force, a melody. The iamb seemed destined to render the rhythms of our epoch, when the world, preparing for dreadful events, was flexing its political and physical muscles. That is why I chose the iambic metre for my poem.

Its theme is the development of the links in a single chain which is a family. Each offshoot develops to a certain degree and is then enveloped by the surrounding society. In each offshoot something individual, new and poignant forms and ripens, at the cost of countless sacrifices, tragedies, falls, defeats, at the cost eventually of losing valuable qualities that are fine and admirable in their season: moral virtues, loyalty, humanity.

In a word, the whirlpool of the world sucks in the man: his personality disappears or lingers in mutilated form, unrecognizable. Once upon a time there was a man. He was no more than a man, nothing but pitiful flesh and a soul shielding its flame. But the seed survived, the grain was scattered, and a son shot out new and stronger shoots. The son disturbed his society, and the whole family, which had been punished by history and its times, began to punish in return; because this last child sometimes knew how to be a lion. He might, with his little hand, catch at the wheel of history. Perhaps it would catch him?

And what then? I don't know, I never knew. I can only say that the concept came to me under the influence of my growing hatred of all theories of progress.

World events have to serve as the basis of three chapters. The first unfolds towards 1878, against the background of the Russo-Turkish war and the early revolutionary movements. In a liberal, cultivated family, the first swallow of individualism arrives, a man with a Byronic face and unknown aspirations, choked back and destroyed by the sickness born at the end of the century.

The second chapter is set at the end of the nineteenth and beginning of the twentieth century. It is devoted to the son of this 'demon', the inheritor of his turbulent aspirations and their unhealthy repercussions. He is the son of our unfeeling century. He is also a link in this family. Nothing remains of this man except a spark he threw into the world – a seed deposited in the womb of a sweet girl one ardent night of love.

In the third chapter the father dies. We know what has become of the brilliant 'demon', into what abyss this extraordinary man has fallen. The action moves from Petersburg to Warsaw. The life of the son ends before the tomb of his father, when he gives way to the third link in this family which has fallen so low though it wished to fly so high.

The epilogue shows us a simple mother, suckling her son, in the middle of the clover-fields of Poland. No one knows her and she herself knows nothing. The boy grows. He begins to talk, and repeats with his mother, 'For you, o my Liberty, I would mount the scaffold!'

This is the last circle of life, the top of the pyramid. Now it is up to him to grow up, to begin to shoulder the world. The offshoot might perhaps be able to hang on to the wheel of history.

The poem must have a leitmotif: the leitmotif of retribution. It is that of the mazurka which successively carries along on its wings Marina, who dreamed of the Russian throne; Kósciuszko, his hand stretched to the sky; Mickiewicz, at balls in Paris and Petersburg.* In the first chapter we hear it from a Petersburg apartment window, in 1870; in the second it bursts out at a ball, which is flooded with the champagne of the *fin-de-siècle*. In the third, it sings in the night, in a snow-storm over Warsaw; it whistles across the fields and prairies of a sleeping Poland. And in its music, eternally recurring and clear, sound the notes of retribution.

Although it is unfinished, this poem counts among Blok's masterpieces. His journey, the obsequies, his posthumous reconciliation with his father worked in him at the deepest level.

'Yes, the son loved the father after all!' he wrote in Chapter Three, and in a letter from Warsaw to Madame Kublitskaya,

> Each day I come to know my father a little better, and he seems to me an extraordinary man, strong and complete. Everything that they tell me about him reveals that he was noble, solitary, that he was high-minded and enlightened. Death, as always, has clarified many things; it has made some sides of him more attractive and blotted out what was no good.

The prologue to the work is in iambics, recalling Pushkin. The nineteenth century, which Blok discusses in the first

---

*Marina, wife of the False Dmitri who was crowned tsar and killed in a rebellion in 1606; Tadeusz Kosciuszko (1746–18170), Polish patriot defeated in battle by the Russians; Adam Mickiewicz (1798–1855), national poet of the Poles, banished to Russia for five years. – Trs.

chapter, is that of the Beketovs, with their simple, hard-working, calm life, with their liberalism, their sympathetic way of thinking and no less appealing way of life. Destruction quickly makes its entrance – stealthy, invisible, still intangible, but already real in its earliest manifestations, both inner and outer. Everything changes, in outward forms of life as well as inside the brains seized by the fever of vain speculations:

> The horn of Roland
> was replaced by the trumpet.

And along comes the twentieth century, the century of comets, of the Messina earthquake, of armaments, of aviation and the death of faith:

> Insuperable disgust with living,
> and love for life in a crazy flood;
> a homeland passion-bound, hate-riven…
> then atrabilious, earthy blood
> that bloats the veins in intimation
> of what? Now all the bounds have been
> overset – unheard-of transformation,
> revolt such as no eye hath seen…

The narrative continues. The 'demon' falls on his prey, like a vulture, and the young girl, who seemed to be going to pass her life peacefully, is torn from the bosom of her family.

In the second chapter, the young hero strolls along the quays of the all-too-blue Neva. He addresses this cursed town, this town which will one day disappear:

> O my elusive town!
> Why did you rise up above an abyss?
> In vain the great-winged Angel*
> lifts a cross above the fortress…
> Flee the treacherous marshes!

*On the spire of the Peter and Paul fortress.

Aleksandr Blok

> Flee this spellbound square
> transparent in the dawn!
> This capital is unknown to me,
> Here a strange dream may appear
> to darken the failing mind...

One hears in this the notes of Pushkin's *Bronze Horseman*, the voices of Gogol and Dostoevsky. Like them, Blok became a poet of Petersburg, of its mystery and extraordinary destiny.

XV

The voyage to Warsaw was difficult. Blok felt ill at ease on the train; he was no longer used to travelling alone and he found it increasingly hard to do without Lyuba.

> I don't need anything, I've taken what I can from this miserable life and don't have the energy to reach for the sky. I was tossed into this railway carriage for Warsaw just as I was tossed into Petersburg. Except she isn't with me to get bored like a child, to shake her little head, doze, laugh, be mischievous.

In Warsaw, where there was much business for him to deal with, he met his father's second wife and his half-sister, a girl of sixteen whom he scarcely knew. He split the inheritance of about 80,000 roubles with her. He had never been greatly concerned about money; when first married, he lived with his mother; in 1907, on Mendeleyev's death, they had received some money and his writings gave them a living. But he'd never had such a sum as this. They could be a little extravagant, plan another trip abroad, buy the old furniture so much admired by Lyuba when she browsed in antique shops.

Blok often moved house, but always remained near the river or a canal, far from the centre and the good neighbourhoods. The water, the islands, the gulf retained the same appeal for him; he liked wandering the back streets, mixing with the dockers and the local factory workers, frequenting squalid cabarets where they served only vodka, beer or tea. Not far away, in the northern suburb of Petersburg, he was often welcomed into the big gypsy restaurants, 'the most agreeable places in the world'.

Little trains took him to the lakes, to Pargolovo and Shuvalovo, pleasant places, summer resorts for the petits-bourgeois, and in winter to magnificent snow-fields where one could ski in complete solitude; the nights seemed even clearer than in the town and the silence more enveloping. Sometimes he went there with the poet Pyast, a failure but a devoted, intelligent and acutely sensitive friend. This man, who became the most tragic of Petersburg figures after the revolution, a fiery and pitiful Don Quixote, left poems that no one can read and two volumes of extremely valuable memoirs. Pyast adored Strindberg; he went to Sweden 'to kiss his footprints, to breathe the air around his house'. But nothing ever worked out for him; when he arrived, Strindberg was dying and would see no one. Sad, disappointed and penniless, Pyast returned to Petersburg. He introduced Blok to the work of the great Swedish writer – it was a revelation.

Angelina, Blok's charming half-sister, a sweet young girl who was to die of tuberculosis during the war, was now living in Petersburg. The memory of his father, whom Blok had hardly known, lived on in him. The students of the Warsaw Law faculty had made a real cult of their former professor, and Blok was surprised and happy to hear the spirited and admiring way in which these young people spoke of the dead sociologist. One collection of late writings appeared, then another, published under the students' aegis; this evidence of esteem and affection deeply touched Blok.

Money rolled in and it was decided to rebuild the Shakhmatovo house, to buy livestock and to change stewards. Shakhmatovo was sacred, it must never disappear, it must always be there and, much as it bored him at this period, Blok didn't want to let it fall apart. His mother and aunt were spending the summer there. Madame Kublitskaya's illness grew worse, her epileptic fits became more and more frequent. Staying in a rest home had led to a brief improvement, but she was pathologically touchy with everyone, especially Lyuba, and it was impossible to live with her.

Blok surrounded her with tenderness and affectionate care. He wrote to her often, keeping her abreast of literary and political life. She was the one he told about his encounters.

> Mama, yesterday a young girl came to see me. It was Hilda.* I was out; she begged to announce her arrival and arrange a meeting with me. I went along out of a mixture of boredom and curiosity. We spent yesterday evening together and the whole of today. Knowing my poems, she came to Petersburg especially to see me. For a year she had been writing me ironic, intelligent letters that turned out to be not at all like her. She is twenty, very lively and very beautiful, morally and physically, and above all, utterly spontaneous. She resembles Hilda even in the smallest details; she speaks just as Hilda would have spoken. We walked and drove, across the town and round the suburbs, to stations and cafés… Today she leaves again…

And in another letter:

> On Saturday I went to Pargolovo, down to the lakes where there was a gypsy concert. I felt my destiny was there. And so it was. The Gypsy Woman sang a song about the many worlds there are and then, in the rain, in the shadows of the night, she told me some extraordinary things. On the station steps she polished her long fingers armoured with sharp rings, and yesterday she was transformed into a purple and blood-coloured sunset (a poem).

He also sent her books and journals. He tried hard to lighten her life, to calm her constantly stretched nerves. But Madame Kublitskaya could no longer control herself; she made the atmosphere oppressive and painful, and when she came to Petersburg there were endless sessions with Lyuba, whom she scolded for her carefree ways, her gaiety, her love of the theatre. Above all, she could not accept Blok's renewed love for his wife – his attraction for so many others, and his passionate flings, she thought natural – nor his vital and ever-increasing need for her. The presence of this

* The heroine of Ibsen's *The Master Builder*.

prematurely aged, morose and nervy mother, who tired
Blok, irritated Lyuba.

Shakhmatovo was now as good as new, but Blok and
Lyuba dreamed of a European trip; they wanted to visit
France, Belgium and Holland. They spent a month in Aber-
Wach, then went to Paris. Even more than in Italy in 1909,
they were agitated by confused and contradictory feelings.
On the one hand it was fine and moving to see 'these old
stones', to 'salute the ruins'. On the other hand, Europe was
not just a museum for them to skim over as tourists. Life was
rumbling on, and what a terrible life! Krupp was increasing
production of armaments; the French could only think of
revenge; the ground was shaking in Portugal and American
tastes and ways were infiltrating Italy, like a young boxer
courting an old noblewoman. The extreme poverty of the
working class and the carelessness of the élite were the
same as in their own 'cursed and dear country'. The rapid
development of the cinema, of the automobile industry, of
aviation, seemed to be the forerunner of a terrible catastrophe – war? barbarism? – which he could not yet define. War
was in the air, it seemed imminent; Europe was ready to
fight.

'Even though we are in Brittany,' he wrote to his mother,

and the life we observe here may be provincial, we are in
Europe, and the life of the world can be felt more strongly than
in Russia. Perhaps because of the press – omnipresent, free,
scathing, talented – perhaps also because in every corner of
Europe mankind is suspended over a precipice ('and gathers
samphire – dreadful trade', as Edgar said, leading the blind
Gloucester), living feverishly, 'by the sweat of his brow'. 'Life
is a terrible monster, happy is he who can stretch out in the
grave' – thus speaks Europe, and no work, no pleasure, can
silence that voice. It is plain that the present civilization is
monstrous and insane. You can see it on the tense faces of the
rich as well as the poor, in the automobile races, in all this life
which has no deep meaning and in the clever, loud, free,
bribed press... All Britain's forces are bent on building ships.

Wilhelm II wants to make war. The French are ready to die for their country… It all resembles a gigantic funfair, stupefying and tiring…

He visited the Louvre several times but couldn't see the *Mona Lisa*, which had just been stolen.

The Louvre is sad and empty. A place made specially for pondering on the budget for the ministries of War and the Navy, which increase every year, while the budget for the Louvre hasn't changed for sixty years. Battleships are the only reason for the disappearance of the *Mona Lisa*.

The 'dear country', as always, welcomed him back with its police and its overcast skies. Disturbing, terrible conversations in the train harried him all night; such conversations were impossible outside Russia.

My country was not slow to show me her divine and bestial face… I wake at dawn. I look out of the window; it is raining. Muddy fields, sparse bushes, a border-guard on a nag, gun over his shoulder. I know exactly where I am. It is she, my unhappy Russia, flecked with the spittle of officials, my dirty, dribbling, numbed country, mocked by the world… Good morning, little mother!

XVI

From his first European trip Blok brought back the *Italian Verses*, from his second a love of old Breton legends, curiosity about the Middle Ages and the idea for a play which was to find its shape later: *The Rose and the Cross*.

There was nothing mystical remaining in his work. Since 1905, a reaction against 'turmoil', 'vagueness', 'imprecision', the 'Romantic' had set in. Over five years, helped by the crisis of Symbolism, Blok had overcome the 'curse of the abstract'. He discovered reality, not Vyacheslav Ivanov's but reality pure and simple, which he found all around him, in his own country and in the world at large, and which affected him in brutal, fertile ways.

In his first years as a poet, everything was merely a symbol to him. He met Bely, and at once they were off down the road together. 'Let us clasp hands / Let us fly into the azure!' But Blok was greater than the reigning poetic schools. If Bely sought inspiration in the writings of German philosophers, and Ivanov in the Greeks, Blok let himself be guided by his own thoughts. He broke with Bely and, after yielding to Ivanov's charm for some time, distanced himself from Ivanov also.

After 1910, the reputation of 'Ivanov's Tower' was in decline. Bely was interested in anthroposophy; Bryusov took a scientific attitude towards his poetry and it became sterile and desiccated. Merezhkovsky and Gippius saw their poetry and prose as conductors of their political and religious ideas. Clear minds began to talk of a crisis in Symbolism. Blok was the only great poet left.

A Symbolist in his early poems – which for some readers remain his most wonderful – Blok can no longer be regarded as such after 1910. He gradually lost that juvenile purity, that mysterious charm, all the mysticism; he was no longer in search of things that would have an affinity with his soul. A year after his marriage he had already formulated his decision not to keep to that obscure path. In his 1906 note-book he wrote: 'Mysticism follows on hysteria', and later: 'The strong soul suffers the mystic crisis without impover-ishment; it does not fear reason. But the weak soul, which does fear reason, has everything to lose... Religion is full-ness. All vague mysticism is emptiness... '

What unexpected words from the mouth of a former Argo-naut! But even more significant are these words from 1910: 'Symbolism, "correspondences", "moments" – all these are mere childishness! We want something else, we are looking for an inner synthesis, a conception of our own world.'

With all his might Blok fought against that 'abstraction', the weight of which he had formerly complained about – it seems as though a new man is speaking:

I am thirty-one, and I feel that I am undergoing a serious crisis. It concerns my conception of the world as much as my poetry. I believe that the last shadow of 'decadence' has dissolved. I want to live. I see in front of me many simple, heady, pleasant possibilities. They are there where I didn't see them before. On the one hand I am a 'social being', that is to say, I really need to communicate with people, at an increasingly deep level, and on the other hand I feel physically so well that I want to take up sport, which must go along with the blossoming of intellec-tual powers. I want massages, and to do gymnastics. I'm crazy about wrestling and physical exercise. All this occupies a quite unexpected place in my life. A year ago I was very far from this. I can read with equal enthusiasm articles on the agricul-tural question and thrillers. They are nearer to Dante than Bryusov is. The brilliant wrestler Van Rihl inspires me much more than Vyacheslav Ivanov. Yes, a real work of art cannot be born these days unless: 1. you maintain real – not cerebral – connection with the universe; 2. our art rubs shoulders with other arts (for me, with painting, music, architecture and gymnastics).*

*Letter to Madame Kublitskaya.

In 1912, he took up the theme again:

> The cruelty of our civilization and all the atheism of modern
> culture are worth more than the ghosts of time past. The
> sanest of men can become a corpse before these invulnerable
> ghosts, yet he will endure monstrous and terrible reality.
> Reality is a necessity. Nothing in the world is more horrible
> than mysticism.

The following year, a propos of literary schools ancient and
modern, he wrote:

> It is time to untie my hands! I'm not a child any more. I answer
> for myself alone. I can still be more lively in myself than the
> 'youths' of the 'middle-aged' generation, weighed down by
> their offspring and their acmeism.*

Neither these diary notes nor the letter to Madame
Kublitskaya written in February 1911 were published
during Blok's lifetime. When they came out in 1932, Bely
was terribly shocked, and spoke of betrayal. And perhaps
he was not entirely wrong; Blok had indeed betrayed 'the
symbolist cause'. But it was only at the price of such betrayal that he could free himself and rise to the ranks of national poets, taking his place alongside Pushkin, Tyutchev and
Lermontov. He became the poet who responded to a whole
people, who drew his poetry from the very springs of his
country, whose destiny he saw and predicted.

Even though he had parted from his comrades-in-arms,
he continued to frequent 'society' – that is, Sologub and the
Merezhkovskys – for which he sometimes felt tenderness
and admiration, sometimes repugnance. During a trip to
Moscow he met Bely again; after 'six years of suffering'
Bely was about to marry a young girl with dreamy eyes and
long ringlets. Blok was reconciled with Sergey very simply;
he had become a priest and was merely a stranger to Blok.

---

*Acmeism: a movement founded by Gumilev and originally called the Poet's
Guild, based on the idea that language has its own structure and logic which
shouldn't be blurred or played around with; opposed both to Symbolism and
Futurism. – Trs.

He felt only indifference towards Bryusov, and the young people who made their literary entrance in the winter of 1911–12 didn't interest him.

He hardly drank at all. Women passed by and left no traces. He himself called these years the dismal years, the grey ones, unfolding too slowly. Nevertheless, during these years his work was fine, rich, deep; it attained an extraordinary perfection. The old legends brought back from France formed the nexus of his play, *The Rose and the Cross*, along with Gaetan's beautiful *chanson*: 'Joy and suffering are one'.

Yet these seemed empty years to Blok. His health was uncertain. Is that why he admired physical strength and sportsmen so much? He suffered from scurvy, and his neurasthenia worried the doctors. He looked after himself, spent much of his time at home, and was bored despite the presence of Lyuba, who had begun to think of the theatre again.

Tolstoy had died, and his death had a great impact. Two currents were clearly distinguishable in Russian literature: one, mainly of prose writers – Andreyev, Gorky – very eclectic in form and imbued with social-democratic (Marxist) ideas. Poets joined in, inheritors of Nekrasov's style, good citizens but mediocre poets. The other, made up of poets and poetic novelists such as Gippius and Sologub, Symbolists and such like, was called 'decadent' by the Marxists. If there were sometimes violent quarrels among the Symbolists, there were none between the Marxists and the 'decadents': they had nothing in common, nothing to say to each other. Andreyev and Gorky had their journals, their audience, their success – great success already.

During these pre-war years, however, it was Blok who was the most loved of all the poets. Balmont's glory was unique; Bryusov's was considerable, but he was very hermetic, and if his famous one-line poem – 'Oh, cover your pale feet' – sent the crowds into ecstasies, his poetry was too difficult for a large public. Blok wrote less than the other two; he made less noise, didn't show off. When he read his poems he looked at nobody, but they listened to him and loved him.

He rarely went to Moscow; the life there, so different from Petersburg, disconcerted him. As five years earlier one would have paired Bely and Blok, now the names of Bely and Bryusov were linked. No one among the latter's followers wanted to admit to his decline. Nevertheless the poetry died out of his verses, killed off by laboratory experiments. The only thing Bryusov sought was a rare rhyme or unusual rhythm. He sacrificed his talent, even his life. The sure, refined taste of his ardent youth had disappeared. He dreamed of writing a book of poems 'of all times and for all people', of uniting in one collection universal pastiches.

Alongside him, Bely remained the poet and theoretician of Symbolism. This extraordinary man, often brilliant and even more often unbearable, and sometimes unreadable, left a precious record of his times. In 1922, in Berlin, he began to write his memoir of Blok. I was close to him at the time; he used to write during the day and in the evening, before making a clean copy, he would read it out to us. He knew how to find the right words in speaking of the poet: humane, intelligent, affectionate. These memories, published in the four issues of *Epopeya* (a Russian journal published in Berlin), were a great literary event. But Bely returned to Russia. Blok's diaries and correspondence were published. Reading certain sections, in which Blok renounced Symbolism and the mysticism of the 'Dawns', annoyed Bely. Dismissing his 1922 memoirs he wrote others, totally distorted. The reader might well hesitate when confronted by two such different accounts. This much is certain: if we want to know Blok as he was seen by Bely, then we must turn to the Berlin memoir; if we want to know Bely as he was in Russia in the years 1930–35, we must read the second memoir. In that, Bely appears as a very unhappy, tormented man, declaring that he had always been a revolutionary of the far Left whom the 'spoilt rich brats' like Blok could only despise. He takes a stand against bourgeois morality. He regrets his youth, during which he wrote articles no one read, wasted in discussions about Kant and

Rickert, while others such as Blok, 'surrounded by adoration since youth', luxuriated in writing verse.

Indeed Bely left many large tomes, *Symbolism*, *Arabesques*, curious, often precious works, dealing with 'symbolism, fetishism, realism, illusionism', the various forms of Russian verse.

From 1907 to 1912 Bely desperately threw himself into the tumult and frenzy of Moscow's literary life: lectures at which students, academicians, society women and political men sometimes heaped him with praise, sometimes laughed him to scorn. Tall, muscular, full of energy and life, he was everywhere, rebellious, fierce and wild, with his windswept hair and his ugly yet handsome face, his mask-like smile, his eyes which were so clear they were almost white. He had no private life, no personal happiness.One day he'd be fighting with Bryusov against the enemies of Symbolism; the next, he'd deliver a speech on neo-Kantianism. He was at all the meetings, the clubs, the newspaper offices, the salons. You couldn't miss him. Hadn't he said one day, 'We're making noise, little brother, we're making noise.'

Yet at the same time a tide of despair was sweeping over him. He wrote *The Silver Dove* and *Petersburg*. One can see the traces of his love for Lyuba in these books, and the drama of his separation from Blok. In *Petersburg*, he is the senator's son. He judges himself harshly. He was never moderate in any sense. 'I have and have always had an idiotic smile,' he said to me once in 1923. He never had any success with women; like all writers he received letters and declarations of love, but his relationships had no future. 'Remember,' he said to me again, 'Andrey Bely has never had a woman he really loved. There was never a woman for Bely.'

Still, he met Assia, a young, pure-faced woman who became his wife. With her he travelled to Africa, to Scandinavia, France and Germany. During the war she left him, and he was never consoled for that. Lyuba and Assia were two names that were never allowed to be pronounced in his presence.

All his feelings were exaggerated. He would nourish a crazy hatred for one person, seeing him as his worst enemy; he would be prepared to give his life for another. Sometimes he was humble, gentle, pure-hearted, pitiable. Then the dreadful grin would return and he would crush things between his fingers; everything would become false and treacherous.

After the break between Blok and Bely years went by, 'years of suffering' for Bely, years that were no less terrible but were otherwise fertile for Blok. In 1909 Bely was staggered to read *On the Field of Kulikovo** and once more approached Blok. A new friendship was formed. Bely went abroad with his wife and sent back many long letters. Obviously it wasn't the friendship, the brotherhood, of the period of 'Dawns'; now certain subjects were taboo, and neither tried to tackle them. Their ways were diametrically opposed, and Bely's growing admiration for Rudolph Steiner, the anthroposophist, was just one more proof of that. But Bely was alone; he needed Blok, who brought him something unique. And Blok loved in Bely his youth, the happiest and most beautiful time of his life.

---

*A poem-cycle written by Blok in December 1908. – Trs.

XVII

During the summer of 1912, Meyerhold and his company gave a series of studio productions in Terioki, a small Finnish seaside resort, two hours by train from Petersburg. The company rented for the season a vast country house, set in a great park. Blok joined his wife there almost every week. They performed Strindberg, Goldoni, Molière, Shaw. Lyubov had major roles; she was happy. She loved the world, gaiety, travel, opera, Wagner, Isadora Duncan's dance recitals, everything that had life and movement. Her happiness was a joy to Blok. He was made much of at Terioki, but felt increasingly tired.

The apartment he was living in now was located in the west of the city, by the Pryazhka canal, a corner somewhat reminiscent of Amsterdam. The Pryazhka, flowing tranquilly between its green banks, had a countrified air. In the summer boys swam in it, but in the winter it was dead calm. There was a fine view from the fourth-storey windows. In the distance the factories, with their tall chimneys and sirens which rent the morning air. Beyond the great docks of the Baltic factories, where the warships were being built, you could see the convent of St Sergius, the distant churches of Gotoyev Island, the tall masts rising from the sea nearby but hidden by the houses opposite. A kilometre away the broad, majestic Neva flowed into the gulf. The masts drew near and retreated. The smell of the port infiltrated everything, the convent bells rang out, the air vibrated. Blok loved this apartment building and remained there until he died. Unhappily, Lyuba was rarely there; she stayed in Terioki, where she was very popular. In Strindberg's play *Guilty – Not Guilty* she took the part of Joanna and was a dazzling success. Blok was the first to admire her. 'Lyuba has found the right voice,' he wrote to his mother, 'her strong, expressive voice matches Strindberg's style perfectly. It was the first time I had heard this language on stage and I was very struck by it. Its simplicity is terrifying. The inner life is translated into mathematical formulae.'

All doors were opening for Meyerhold, who worked at the Imperial Theatre in Petersburg and whose talent as a director was widely applauded. Strindberg's play was a success; the daughter of the Swedish writer, passing through Terioki, made Blok and Lyubov's acquaintance.

When Lyuba had a few days free, she went to Petersburg where Blok impatiently, happily awaited her. He prepared himself for their meeting, he bought flowers, one might say he put his soul in order. She arrived, vivacious and joyful; they dined together gaily and chatted late into the night. 'Tonight, because Lyuba has a sore throat and is staying in her room, I brought home chocolates and cakes and fireworks to amuse her – sparklers, snakes etc.'

But often he waited in vain:

> A very painful thing has happened to me. Lyuba betrayed me. After my letter of the 23rd and her words, I might have expected her today or at least hoped for a telegram from her, announcing her arrival. It's already three o'clock; I've waited in for her all morning and lost the day. I don't know how to reclaim it.

Night fell. The glow of bonfires turned the sky purple, bonfires often lit by riotous groups in the shipyards. From the *Condé*, which had just arrived with French ministers, salvoes sounded.

This mysterious tiredness continued to grow; his body retained its youthful, healthy appearance but he felt that some illness was gnawing away at him. He lay down for hours on end, following the buzzing flies with a distracted gaze. Precious hours were lost and he could not pull himself together. 'The day passes / In a mild madness.'

His mornings, which began late, were devoted to reading. He read masses of newspapers with their mixed tidings: reaction, revolution, the threat of war, the stupidity of

European diplomacy, arrogant and perfidious Germany, proud, short-sighted France, indecisive and hostile Britain! Then, a lot of journals – Merezhkovsky was preaching in the desert. An instinct for self-preservation pushed Bryusov nearer the Futurists, who nevertheless ignored his pressing advances. The extreme Right kept repeating their dated slogans and saw hanging as the safeguard of tsarism. He had a great deal of post every day: letters from publishers, deadly dull. Bely asked for his support of a new journal he was to edit. He wanted to revive the true Symbolism of 1904; with Blok and Vyacheslav Ivanov, he hoped to hold his head high before all the world.

'My dear Boris,' Blok replied on 25 January 1912,

> our letters have crossed – such a nuisance. Even when I am in good health, I find it difficult to keep myself in check; and if I had been able to see you, I would have preferred to see you alone, without Ivanov, whom I like very much but who is very far from me at present. You are thinking of founding a journal. I feel less ready than ever for such a venture. I can send you articles, but no more. At the moment I feel very much alone and, above all, I'm afraid of a trio (with V.I.). Besides, many things frighten me. I am very much alone.
>
> In the letter I wrote you from Moscow, I explained why, even when healthy, I would have hesitated to see you. I told you that I was obsessed with Strindberg... As always, I write very little; I have to struggle against the heavy indifference of recent times. Nevertheless, I will try to write something for your journal... Let me have your Petersburg address. I wish you would see Pyast. Through him you would know the circle of people around me. That is indispensable for us both. The atmosphere around Ivanov at present is unbearable to me.

He had to reply to all his post, and some days he wrote as many as eight letters; he was also correcting the proofs of his third volume of poems, soon to appear from the Moscow publishing house Musaget, with which Bely was involved. With effort and difficulty he revised several poems which, however, count among his best work. The form is simple, the verse melodious. He used certain words in such a way that they became 'his', and his rhythms were so individual that they were sufficient to identify the author. Blok's poetry of the years 1908 to 1914, in its form and content, was profoundly influential on two generations.

But the days continued, 'with their banal work / And petty cares'. He often lunched with his mother, who remained ill and very difficult. Then the procession of intruders would begin: artists in search of advice, poets who came to read their verses to him, or his sister Angelina, of whom he was fond but who trailed behind her the heavy atmosphere of the petite-bourgeoisie which he so loathed. Women harassed him, too, with declarations, reproaches, scenes... He detested this feminine idiocy, this pathological self-centredness, this sentimentality, this 'soul blindness', and decided to put an end to such wearing relationships. 'Everything is known in advance, nothing but trouble. Neither they nor I need all that.' And they were all the same, whether sixteen or thirty. What demands, what a waste of time!

In the late afternoon he went out; he went for a walk or called in at the offices of the children's magazine, edited by Vladimir Solovev's sister, to which he contributed; he was pleased by the pedagogical ideas of this original woman. And he often had to listen to the Acmeist poets in fashionable salons. Grouped around their leader, Gumilev, the Acmeists declared that everything was simple, that words meant what they said and no more. Blok loathed their theories and their glossy journal, *Apollon*. Other young people – ego-Futurists, Futurists – noisy nuisances, were beginning to make themselves heard. He felt further and further away from it all.

He returned on foot. The workers were coming out of the factories, buying vodka and quickly emptying the bottles right there in the street; one of them was beating a little girl. He crossed the good neighbourhoods; on the Nevsky Prospekt an elegant crowd, richly dressed, fur-coated, jewelled, double-chinned, stared blankly. 'If you undressed them, a bloodless, corrupt, soiled, violated corpse would appear.' At home the same thoughts obsessed him. The cook and the housemaid lived in an ignorance and vulgarity that frightened him.

> My blood freezes with shame and despair. There is nothing but emptiness, spitefulness, blindness, misery. Only absolute compassion could lead to change. Our bourgeois apartments with their doors well padlocked are even worse. I react in this way because I don't have a clear conscience... I know what I ought to do: give up all my money, ask forgiveness of every-one, give away my books, my clothes... but I cannot, I don't want to...

A few friends joined him for dinner. They chatted, discussed Bryusov's latest article.

> It is sad, cold, accurate and yet touching, this review of my poems by Bryusov. In between the lines you can read, 'Oh well, comrade! One is bored? One would like to catch the bluebird by the tail?' Yes, I'm bored. Is it possible for life to pass by this way? Reading, writing, receiving letters, writing them, correcting proofs! No, it would be better 'to go for a stroll in the woods with a cosh'.*

He said goodbye to his friends, or went out with them. After putting in a brief appearance at some discussion group about literature or politics or religion, a cab would whirl him away to a restaurant or music-hall.

> An acrobat emerges from the Variety. I implore her to come with me. We roll on through the night as deep as an abyss. I am beside myself. I don't know whether we are still in the first cab or whether this is the second. All night she keeps her hand over her mouth. I tear her lace. In her rough hands, her pointed nails, there is a mystery, a force. Hours with her, distressing, unavailing. I take her back. There's something sacred, as though she were a child, my daughter. She disappears down an

---

* Popular song.

alleyway. ...Everything is black. Petersburg is the most terrible and the most captivating of towns, it reinvigorates the blood more than any other town in Europe.

At dawn the first newspapers come out. The *Titanic* has sunk. An exhilarating, malicious joy rises up in him. 'So it still exists, this eternal Ocean!'

The day breaks. Certainly no one around him sees what slope Russia is sliding down, with all its literature, and himself along with it!

To another letter from Bely he replies: 'Above the sad men, above sad, ragged Russia, Vyacheslav Ivanov rattles a thunder-sheet... We must show people our true face, sad and human, and not the mask of a non-existent school of literature.'

He was not fair to Ivanov, however, who with all his skills and shrewdness was fighting against the Acmeism Blok himself rejected. But Blok did not understand the fight; he wanted nothing to do with it. He knew that for the 'best' (Bely, Remizov), as for himself, there was no viable outcome, that 'those nearest are on the threshold of madness'.

'I know what must be done,' he said, 'but it is still too soon to leave this world – so beautiful and so terrible.' Everything disgusted him, horrified him: faces in the street and on trams, the face of his housemaid:

> I've seen her, I've heard her voice. It's something impossible, frightful. At first sight she is just a girl like any other, but that raucous voice coming from her toothless mouth! What is most terrible is the mixture of human and animal forms. It often occurs. That's why I hate going to Shakhmatovo. One can put up with syphilis, but only in a human form. What I have seen is unbearable. Just like that general, his neck in rolls of fat. It is all due to degeneration: it is horrifying because here the 'human' mingles with the 'alien'.

Ugliness made him suffer, and yet he met it everywhere. Everything around him was dirty, hideous, horrific. Here a body, fished out of the water, there a filthy little beggarwoman, coughing, a bit further on, a tramp drinking dirty water from streams.

Fortunately, Lyuba was there. She arrived, full of her theatre stories. He listened, enchanted, he was seized by a desire to see her on stage without her suspecting his presence. She told him that everything wasn't going smoothly, that the pantomimes brought in 300 roubles a night but Goldoni only 30; she spoke of Meyerhold and his new ideas. But then Blok became belligerent: he tried to explain that the 'moderns' separated them, that they were empty, that they had no grasp of the truth. Did he really think so, or was he moved by jealousy? Everything related to Lyuba's theatrical life made him touchy. He maintained that Meyerhold was an artistic opportunist, which greatly saddened Lyuba. 'I should love to live, if I knew how,' he cried. She didn't understand him. He told her what the whole town gossiped about, that friends were asking whether they intended to divorce.

Yet she was there! He didn't want to think about anything, he was no longer alone, they were together and he was happy. And one evening, instead of writing a poem for Lyuba as he so often did, he copied into his diary a poem by Karolina Pavlova (1810–79):

> You are all the heart is pleased by,
> Everything the mind holds near;
> You are my strength, you are my true love –
> May your sleep be sweet, my dear!
>
> You are my strength, you are my true love,
> And your light shines on my way,
> My whole life, my destiny.
> May your sleep be sweet, my dear!
>
> My whole life, my destiny,
> Life has passed me by in vain,
> You, who are my youthful folly,
> May your sleep be sweet, my dear!

Destiny has now united
Everything in one bright star,
A single image, piercing midnight.
May your sleep be sweet, my dear!

XVIII

Inspired by the old legends of Brittany and Languedoc, Blok's play *The Rose and the Cross* was initially intended as the scenario for a ballet for which Glazunov would write the music. Then the plan was altered; Blok thought of an opera and began to work along those lines. But on reading it, his mother and friends protested that *The Rose and the Cross* was a play not an opera; the character of Bertrand was essentially dramatic. Blok was persuaded and rewrote his work, changing the tone and the ending, which didn't please him.

It was then that Remizov introduced him to Mikhail Tereshchenko,* an intelligent, cultured and immensely rich young man who became an enlightened Mycenas for young writers and poets. Tereschenko wanted to publish a journal and set up a publishing house to help Remizov, Sologub, Bely and Blok win over a larger public. His two energetic and enthusiastic sisters helped him in this work.

Full of zeal, Tereshchenko was reluctant to leave his new friends; he took Remizov and Blok in his car to dine on the Islands. In the evenings the collaborators met, chatted gaily, argued, and various projects were initiated. Blok appreciated this refreshing friendship, which brought him comfort and reassurance. Pressed by Tereschenko, encouraged by Remizov, he finished *The Rose and the Cross*.

The subject is very simple: the hapless Bertrand, the 'knight of sorrows', loves Izora, the châtelaine, to whom a young page – an audacious admirer – pays court. But all Izora thinks about is a troubadour, of whom she knows

---

*Mikhail Ivanovitch Tereshchenko (1886–1956), owner of the publishing house Sirin, which published Bely's *Petersburg*. He was a close collaborator of Kerensky in the Provisional Government, in which he was first Minister of Finance and then of Foreign Affairs.

nothing except a single song. Her heart is full of him and she wants to find him. The magnanimous Bertrand goes off in search of him; he travels all over Brittany and finds Gaetan, the author of Izora's song. But it is an almost blind old man that he brings back to Languedoc.

A tournament is organized at the château. Izora knows that her troubadour, the man who sings 'Joy and suffering are one', is near her. The tournament begins with a minstrel singing a war song; then, after a love ballad, Gaetan gives his song. Izora sees him and understands that all her waiting has been in vain. The Knight of Sorrows knows that his Lady will never love him; at night he helps the young page to get into her chamber, and then dies beneath her window.

Tereshchenko was thrilled by *The Rose and the Cross*; Blok became even dearer to him. They had lengthy discussions about the possibility of staging the play. Blok, slightly in love with one of Tereshchenko's sisters, found in these gifted, fervent, sympathetic young people an understanding he greatly needed. Of course he remained withdrawn, and indeed still avidly sought 'fleeting encounters'. But there was so much amusement and liveliness in Mikhail Tereshchenko's company! As Blok was not materially dependent on him, their friendship could be of the freest kind. By this time a new passion had replaced that for the circus: Blok was now enthusiastic about roller-coasters, was drawn to them, marvelled at them. He wanted Tereshchenko to share in this passion and dragged him off to Luna Park. In this noisy, sad place they carried on very serious conversations.

> We talked about art and religion. Tereshchenko has never been religious and he thinks that everything that religion can give, art is able to give him. I replied by developing this idea; that there is an infinity in art; we do not know any longer what is the end of art, why it exists or what it means; it is empty and dangerous. Religion, on the other hand, does have an end; one finds richness and salvation in it. He also asked me whether I

would like to bring back those moments when art opened up the infinite for me. No, even if it were possible, I can't wish for that. What is at the very boundaries of art cannot be loved. I told him that I had once known things that were greater than art; that is, not the infinite but an End, not worlds but the Universe. I have probably lost that for ever; I have denied, I have betrayed, I have fallen very low. Now I am merely an *artist*, and I live not for what gives fullness to life but for what makes it black, repellent, disgusting.

But where and how could *The Rose and the Cross* be performed? They thought of Diaghilev, and then Blok decided to read his play to Stanislavsky. Thus began the long and painful series of attempts made to stage the play. Used to a realist, psychological theatre, Stanislavsky was not taken with the work, which is more of a poem than a theatrical play. Yet he didn't reject it; for a year Blok kept hoping, but time went by and nothing happened. In 1916 he was called to Moscow; the players learned their parts, the final details were settled and Blok was happy. But the 1917 revolution put an end to all such projects.

Blok was deeply distressed. From his first meeting with Stanislavsky he understood that he was confronted by a man from another world, whose character and temperament would not permit him to understand Blok. His own feelings about the theatre were contradictory enough. At the time of *The Puppet Booth*, nothing surpassed Meyerhold's modern theatre; in 1912 – because of Lyuba – he repudiated it. The Moscow Art Theatre surprised and disconcerted him with its outdated, old-fashioned ways, and left him unmoved. In 1919 Blok was to return to the theatre, but this time in order to earn a living.

Remizov's and Sologub's works appeared from Tereshchenko's publishing house. Bely, in Moscow, was hard at work on a novel, but financial worries overwhelmed him and prevented his finishing it. Blok, on learning of his friend's embarrassment, sent him 500 roubles and convinced Tereshchenko that he should publish *Petersburg*, one of the world's most extraordinary prose works to appear before the First World War.

Blok and Tereshchenko haunted the bookstalls; they had discovered a sudden passion for eighteenth- and nineteenth-century first editions, and ferreted through everything in the hope of unearthing one. Every one of the little shops on Vasilyevsky Island was minutely searched! But summer was approaching, Tereshchenko left Petersburg, Blok and Lyuba planned to spend a month on the Basque coast. And when Lyuba wanted something, everything became clear, simple, easy.

At Guéthary life unfolded lightly, quickly, happily. They bathed, and rode horses. The air and the sea had a particular, unfamiliar tang. Nature was generous, people carefree and the sun bountiful and warm. How difficult it was to leave such captivating, wonderful things! But Lyuba had a theatre engagement and Blok had pressing obligations. He had to return.

A new love awaited him.

In Petersburg operas were performed in two theatres: the Mariynsky Opera House and the Musical Drama Theatre. The programmes were almost the same, but in the Musical Drama Theatre the settings were more modern, the singers younger and their style different. This was a very fashionable theatre; its public was less sophisticated and more serious than that at the Imperial Theatre.

Mlle Delmas was playing there. She was a much-applauded Carmen. Tall, thin, red-haired, green-eyed, she had an extraordinary appeal. As soon as he saw her, Blok fell in love. Merimée's story and Bizet's music were combined in a blazing, passionate, bewitching figure, driving away the gypsy impressions. Her shoulders, her proud bearing, her flaming hair and above all her beautiful voice, grave and warm, inspired him to ardent, sad poetry. One section of the third volume, *Carmen*, is devoted to this alluring, dazzling woman, with whom he was madly in love for two years. Blok's poems make her out to be an original, cruel *femme fatale*; she was in fact quite different. She remained with

Blok until he died; she became a tender, devoted friend to him, and her beauty, calm, simplicity, equilibrium and almost maternal care soothed many a torment. The 'fiery Spaniard' became the guardian angel.

This love, so unlike previous loves, made one thing painfully clear to Blok: he was no longer young. The love for Volokhova: gypsies, madness, music, white nights, storms, break-ups! Now a calmed passion became a faithful friendship, and his exalted verses were a curious response to peaceful walks and tranquil evenings in Mlle Delmas's company, her keen intelligence divining and understanding all that was painful and complicated in Blok's.

Carmen is only a small part of his third collection. A new and quite different theme appeared in the poetry of the years 1908 to 1914: Russia.

'My bond with the world has been strengthened,' said Blok in 1912. And this was true.

XIX

Blok's third volume was the greatest and most beautiful volume of Russian poetry to appear since the death of Tyutchev in 1873. No poet had attained such profundity of thought, such perfection of form, such an accent of sincerity. His upright, noble nature, his fertile genius, his passion for truth created masterpieces.

A horror of life and a love of it, disgust at human beings and attraction to them, the vanity of art and its necessity — all this mingled in him and tore him apart; his agonies were intense. There was a poison in the magic of this verse; it obsessed the strong and crushed the weak. Blok glided along the road of his age, and it became increasingly clear that at the end there would be nothing but mud, dust and grief.

Religion had died in Blok with the cult of the Beautiful Lady. Perhaps he retained a scrap of faith, but everything mystical was anathema to him. Even in his second volume several notes emerge that prepare us for his last poems. He took the first step towards clarity, he discovered real life and enveloped himself in total pessimism.

But it was only one step, a hesitant attempt. Vagueness remained, the romantic veil was still intact, and where Blok's voice rang out free of all artifice, the thought and style were still imperfectly formed.

Now everything was changed. The Virgin of the Rainbow, the Unknown Woman of seedy cabarets, disappeared. He knew that the City – the ghost town of *The Night Watches*, with its quays and marble, its tsar and terrorists – was only a mirage, indeed the whole country was a mirage, and that he himself, with his despair, his boredom, his dreams, his sickness, was merely a ghost, one of the last – perhaps the very last – of this period of Russian history.

This feeling of being intimately and irrevocably linked to

world events and to the destiny of his country was not new. Blok had already experienced it during the Symbolist era – that concept of the world, that marvellous gift offered to him one fine day by Bely. Then all had been harmonious and unified. An earthquake in the Philippines, red clouds in the sky over Shakhmatovo, an automobile speeding through the streets of Petersburg, a tango danced in Paris – everything merged, had one meaning, inspired the same terror and the same wonder. From this period Blok always retained an attraction to the underside of the world, a desire to know what was going on behind appearances.

Now his theme had become the theme of his native land, of the age. The laws of space and time weighed heavily on him. He was far from Vyacheslav Ivanov, who was lost in the refined elaboration of his 'Symbolist' thought; far from Bely, who was totally absorbed in the anthroposophy of Rudolf Steiner, and was trying to combine in a new philosophy the ideas of the German professor with those of Goethe and Solovev, with the music of Beethoven and Wagner and even with eurythmic dancing. Far, too, from the young – Acmeists, Futurists – who were moved by a wild desire for simplification, who wished either to give back to words their original meanings, and thus called for images not reasoning, or for a direct style of virile, resonant voices with simple, healthy thoughts. Far from Bryusov, who was lost in the subtleties of form, and from Merezhkovsky, who felt himself to be 'above all that'.

Russia replaced the Virgin and the prostitute; that humble, drunken Russia, maligned yet adored, whose son he was and whose fate he must share. She was 'Galilee' for him, 'the unresurrected Christ'. What did it matter, Galilee or the field of Kulikovo? She engulfed him, she absorbed him. With a mixture of fatalism, horror, sensuality, he gave himself up to her, lost himself in her. With her, 'the impossible became possible'; they were together until death, linked forever in a bottomless sadness, sharing the same destiny:

> But oh, my lowly homeland,
> would you tell my heart your meaning?
> And oh my love, poor wife,
> why all this bitter keening?

The idea of a possible separation blossomed for a moment.

> Oh, for a change of direction, heart, company...
> what has your gloom to attract a free soul?*

But he knew that he could never bring himself to do it; after all, what would be left for him?

> Still more cunning, glory, money,
> flattery – the crown of all -
> man's stupidity, that towers
> inescapable, triumphant,
> infinite. Will that be all?

> No... there's forest yet, and clearings,
> villages, the broad highway,
> our own Russian road, the touch
> of our own Russian mist at evening,
> breezes rustling in the hay.

She alone existed, but he hadn't managed to render her face. In 1913 he already saw her surrounded by wooden crosses. Who was she? The factories smoked, the filthy hovels reeked, the thatched villages flamed. He knew that all this would disappear, that something else would come. But what? A new world? Then this life would seem a dream, as the Tatar hordes had come to seem. What part would he play? He had no idea. For the moment, he was alone with her.

And it is difficult to imagine a more profound isolation! Without friends, because he had nothing in common with his 'brother writers', his neighbours in the literary guides of the twentieth century; without a wife, because his true

---

*Translated by Jon Stallworthy and Peter France: Alexander Blok, *Selected Poems* (Harmondsworth: Penguin, 1974), p. 82.

wife, fatefully bound to him, obstinately hid her face. He tried to work it out: was he divine, marked by suffering? Or was he nothing but the horrible mouth of some repellant animal? His health deteriorated, his spirit wavered; he no longer recognized himself.

> I myself am not the man I once was –
> Inaccessible, baleful, pure and proud.
> More goodwill and less hope in tomorrow
> Take me down this tedious, simple road.

Until life crushed him he would remain proud and pure, but the struggle would be terrible.

Blok's poetry, taken together, looks like the development of a conception of life within love. It is a long path from the religious lyricism of the poems to the Beautiful Lady to the echoes of street-songs in his late work, from Vladimir Solovev, his first master, to Apollon Grigoriev, the companion of his last years. The feminine images reflect different aspects of his amorous experiences. The adolescent who prostrated himself before the Eternal Feminine became, ten years later, a man who abandoned himself to explosive, devouring passions. More ecstasy and fervour, but storms in the heart, unbridled fits of rage, heavy, drunken despair, the spirit torn and a sense of degeneration:

> I hide nothing from you.
> Look at me!
> Here I stand, burnt by the flames
> Of the blazing fires of hell.

What led Blok from the 'ideal of the Madonna' to the 'ideal of Sodom'? A thirst for the infinite, for unknown sensations, for intensity, for the absolute. One truth intoxicated and guided him: the soul is immortal and cannot be satisfied with temporal, finite joys. The soul, poisoned by innumerable desires, knows that only the satisfaction of these desires can appease its thirst for the infinite. Confronted by this greed, this expectation of the impossible, everyday life becomes weary and intolerable.

In 1908 he had already sensed Russia's sorrowful destiny. Political questions didn't interest him, only the preservation of the essence of his country's immortal soul, and the future, which he saw as an unrelenting struggle to defend the eternal elements of that soul. He was obsessed by this theme, not as a thinker with abstract reasoning, but as a poet who feels, suffers and loves. Russia was the new incarnation of the Eternal Feminine. He sees her first 'eternally clear'; then her features become wild, chaotic, impassioned, tormented, beautiful, curiously reminiscent of *Faina* and *Carmen*. He begins to talk of a 'fatal country', of her 'drunken voice', of her beauty, like that of a gypsy. And he arrives at *The Twelve*. It was not political ideas that inspired him in this poem, but the spirit of this popular rising, which he had lived so intensely and which he had to judge: was it for God or against God? He who was always ready 'to trample on things cherished and sacred', who made fun of 'the dock-tailed constitution', who detested 'ladies in astrakhan', approved of the events of 1905 and 1917. 'The landscape of his soul', too, was made up of wind, snow-storms, wild horizons. For a long time he had experienced the boredom of the assassin after his crime.*

Blok was the creator of a new style that was entirely his own. His metaphors are incomparably beautiful and his metaphorical neologisms daring and original. He composes sets of metaphors which fit together, link up and become a metaphorical theme, a poetic reality. These metaphorical developments sometimes end up in catachreses (disagreeing with the original metaphor) which, repudiated in classical poetry, largely contributed to the richness of Romantic poetry. As much as illogical truths, he liked – and often used – dissonances.

The principal feature of Blok's poetry, however, is the musical point of departure of each of his poems. He hears them as a harmony of sound, and is not afraid to sacrifice

---

*See *The Twelve*, VIII. (The reference to the constitution concerns that guaranteed by the October Manifesto of 1905 but soon curtailed; those who believed in it were mocked in 'The Poets', a poem written by Blok in 1908. – Trs.)

words in the interests of preserving the sonority so dear to him.

In this poetry, which people continue to call 'Symbolist', there is nevertheless no traditional Symbolism. The mass of little themes, in harmony with the main theme, form a complete ensemble. This ensemble often touches the limit of the real, and if symbols exist, they become accessory to a landscape, bringing us the presentiment or the aftertaste of another reality in which the poet moved more easily than in the first.

Since Lomonosov (1711–65), Russian poetry has had its tonic metre: twelve-foot iambic (which corresponds to the alexandrine), decasyllabic, eight-foot iambic (the most popular metre) and so forth. The nineteenth-century poets almost all followed the rules of tonic verse. Bryusov, Gippius and Sologub were the first to break with this metre. Bely and Blok created new, virtuoso rhythms: on the one hand they refined the iambic, bringing it to a supreme perfection; on the other they shattered this same classical iambic, introducing pauses, paeons and spondees. These innumerable combinations provided a rich resource for modern rhythms.

In his third volume, Blok returned to a certain classicism of form and rhyme. There, too, he worked in two directions: he gave classical rhyme a degree of extreme refinement but also, breaking with tradition, he introduced a great deal of assonance into Russian poetry. That which he brought to perfection, he immediately destroyed, so varied and rich were his means.

Anna Akhmatova and Mayakovsky – in their own ways – benefited from this de-canonization of rhythm, of rhyme and of all the old prosody. Blok contributed hugely to the development of vocabulary, and modern poetic language owes its unparalleled richness to his example.

XX

The war caught Blok at Shakhmatovo. He greeted it as a new absurdity in a life already absurd. He loved Germany – the Germany of universities, poets, musicians and philosophers; he wasn't at all sure why people had to fight each other for their leaders' pleasure. The hardest and most shameful peace was, for him, more worthwhile than any war. Lyuba immediately sat for a nursing diploma and was sent off to the front. Mikhail Tereshchenko gave up all literary activity.

During this first winter of the war, Acmeism was increasingly successful. One cannot deny that it attracted talented poets, but to Blok the movement recalled Bryusov's poetic principles: it reeked of the laboratory. Gumilev, the head of the young movement, was less an adversary than a stranger, someone whom it was impossible for Blok to understand. With the exception of Anna Akhmatova, who had great poetic talent, and of Osip Mandelstam, an extraordinarily gifted and original poet, Gumilev's followers were totally lacking in personality. Blok was hostile to Acmeism, and even more so to the famous journal *Apollon*, which he thought the height of snobbishness.

> An article by Gumilev concerning the new poetic practice has been published in *Apollon*. He says that symbolism is dead and that a new school has appeared, which must be a worthy successor to its defunct father. Gumilev hardly mentions what, for us, is an invaluable truth. He doesn't seem to know that our school, although it bears the same name as the French school of poetry, was closely bound up with questions of philosophy, religion and social matters. It had gone as far as it could by about 1913, but not for the reasons Gumilev gives. The real reason was that by that time the symbolists were

surrounded by parasites who were trying to sell off, at ridiculous prices, things that were extremely precious and significant to us. On one side Bryusov and his school compressed religion and philosophy into a scholastic framework; on the other, the 'street' burst into poetry and began to vulgarize it. So the discussions came to an end; the temple emptied; the treasures – not only purely literary ones – were carried away by what was then a very small band. Each retreated into his corner, sad, silent and solitary. It was then that Gumilev came along. He brought a new idea: acmeism. But the one idea he'd ever had he took from me. Two years previously, Vyacheslav Ivanov and I had discussed the future of Russian poetry and it was actually I who put forward the idea in that same *Apollon*.

Thus he fought, albeit half-heartedly, with the young. But the magic of his poetry was such as to render any polemic futile. Except perhaps for Mayakovsky – who considered Bely, Blok and Sologub to be corpses – no one could escape his influence, and the young Acmeists less than the others. Occasionally even Blok appreciated their reaction against Symbolism:

> On the literary front, a clearing of the air. Painful and cheering. People do not seem to understand or care for symbolism any more. Soon they will not seem to care for art. Religion and art are dying. We are heading for the catacombs. They despise us all, irrevocably. The worst persecution is indifference. Fortunately, after that we will be stronger and fewer.

The apartment on the Pryazhka canal was no longer as lively as it had been. Lyuba was at the front; many friends were away. Petersburg was mournful and dreary. Blok's notebook is full of sad jottings:

> It is the end for Petersburg.

> When will I be free to put an end to myself?

And, a little later:

> There was once a man and a woman; they made each other
> unhappy. The wife said to the husband: 'It's impossible to live
> like this. You are the stronger – go and find a string and pull it,
> so that the world changes.'

He began to understand that 'a war is never great. It is a vast
factory on the move, that's its real meaning.'

He was pained by Lyuba's absence and thought of her all
the time. 'I haven't had a hundred, two hundred, three
hundred women or more. I have had two. One is Lyuba, the
other – all the others. They were different and I too was
different.'

Still, Mlle Delmas came to see him almost every day, and
Petersburg was always beautiful.

> I took a river-boat and went for a trip on the Neva. I saw that
> Petersburg is only German-Jewish in the centre. The outskirts
> are majestic and very Russian. After the Smolny [a former
> convent] the enormous grain warehouses begin, the lines of
> merchant wagons, the green banks, the gigantic domes; one
> sees the tugboats – *Prophet*, *Liberty*. The waves were very
> high, the Neva blue and wide; above her I saw a rainbow.

It was fifty years since the death of Apollon Grigoriev, and
Blok wanted to take advantage of his anniversary to revive
the memory of this forgotten poet. Enthusiastically, he set
about preparing an edition of his complete works, but the
task was interrupted by a trip to Moscow: Stanislavsky
asked him to come in connection with staging *The Rose and
the Cross* at the Arts Theatre. But it was in vain that
Germanova and Gzovskaya quarrelled over the role of
Izora; the play, too alien to Stanislavski's concept of theatre,
was never to be performed.

Moscow had greatly changed in the war. There was talk
of mobilizing Blok's age-group. The Futurists were writing
patriotic poems. The air was heavy. They were better
informed than in Petersburg about what was unfolding in
the corridors of the Duma, about the government's instabil-
ity and the losses at the front.

In July 1916 Blok was called up. He had written very little during the year; from time to time he took up fragments of *Retribution* but mostly he idled, waiting for the events he sensed were approaching. What events? Every day the newspapers brought a great deal of contradictory news, but he wasn't waiting for that. A separate peace? He did not hide it: it was his dream. The end of the tsarist regime? That had to come, and although he did nothing to hasten that end, Blok sincerely desired the fall of the Romanovs. The army's victories and retreats left him cold, and when he was called up he had the feeling of becoming one functionary among a crowd of others.

He was attached to a unit of two thousand sappers about ten kilometres from the front. This life, so different from that which he had always led, didn't trouble him too much. In the requisitioned castle where he was billetted with ten officers, they drank, played chess, rode horses half the day, criticized the bad food and the incompetence of the commanders, and were very bored. In this small corner of white Russia, lost amid marshes and thick woods, the winter was cold and dark, the spring rainy and the summer torrid. The guns thundered. Petersburg was far away. The sluggish post brought no exciting news. Lyuba had an engagement with a travelling theatrical troupe. Madame Kublitskaya, very ill, had been taken to a clinic; his stepfather, promoted to general, was fighting in Galicia. Interminable columns went by, some on their way up to the front, others coming back. The telegraph chattered incessantly; behind a partition men played the mandolin around the smoking stove. One day Adjutant Alexei Tolstoy, future author of *Peter the Great*, stopped in this lost outpost. Blok was glad to meet him, but Tolstoy went on his way the same evening and Blok remained alone in the snowy night, beside the turning sails of the old windmills.

At the end of February 1917 a telegram from Petersburg announced the revolution, the tsar's abdication and the formation of a provisional government with Mikhail Tereshchenko as Minister of Finance. Blok, wild with joy and full of hope, asked for a pass and made his way to Petersburg.

The tonic, intoxicating news burst over a celebrating city. The war was far away. And for the first time Blok, who had suffered from a terrible sense of isolation all his life, felt that he was in total communion with the people around him. A strong and precious bond united him to these strangers whom he believed to be very distant from him and whom he sometimes feared; now he shared their joys and hopes and felt ready to share their struggles and suffering. These people were no longer the drunken carter from Shakhmatovo, who beat his wife and swore to set fire to his master's house; no longer the tramp slaking his thirst in the dirty water of the stream, nor the dead, animal face of his maid. It was *another people*, awakened, strong, aware, those whom he had always hoped to know and love, from whom he felt ready to beg forgiveness for his past life. His heart beat stronger and faster, he was animated. On street corners, in the rooms full to bursting at the Winter Palace, he admired the people who crunched sunflower seeds and listened avidly to the speakers. How far he felt from Tereshchenko, Minister of Finance! His hatred of the liberals increased, he voted with the people, he expected the socialists to end the war and begin a new life.

But his hopes were very quickly disappointed. His joy and his passion subsided. The Russian socialists, like their French and British comrades, wanted to beat Germany above all. And Blok found himself alone once again with his desire for peace, alone with his sudden disquiet and the first presentiment of catastrophe.

Life unravelled with astonishing rapidity. Jam-packed trains ran irregularly; the post was increasingly fitful; the food supply diminished. But how beautiful the city was that spring of 1917! The swarming city, decked out in red, vibrant with revolutionary songs, drunk on hope! Trucks covered in flowers went to and fro, bearing pictures of Kerensky, the first love of the Russian revolution.

'It is sweet to live in this gloomy, solitary abyss called

Petersburg in the year 1917, in Russia in the year 1917!' he wrote in May and, a few days later: 'The tragedy has not yet begun.' He was disoriented after his time in Pinsk and hadn't found his way of life again. From several posts suggested to him, he chose that of reporter to the Extraordinary Investigatory Commission appointed to inquire into unlawful acts committed by tsarist ministers.

A new life began, made up – as he said later – 'of meetings on a planetary scale'. The Commission sat every day; Blok took down the verbatim reports of the ministers and collaborators of the tsarist regime imprisoned in the Peter-Paul Fortress. He often went with the examining judges – all new, voluntary workers – into the cells where all the rot of the old regime left him puzzled, full of disgust and of pity. These prisoners – some hateful, others brave and resolute, yet others former dandies who had no idea what was happening – roused in him a crowd of complex and painful feelings. And if on some days he felt ready to demand the death penalty for the entire old guard, on others, he wrote:

> My heart is soaked with tears of pity for all of it, for all. Remember: one should never judge. Remember the words of Klimovich in his cell, and how he said them; the tears of old Kafafov, the sobs of Beletsky during his interrogation, swearing how ashamed he felt of his own children… Tomorrow I shall see these people again. I see them in distress and humiliation. I didn't see them in their splendour and in 'the glory of power'. One has to watch them with intense concentration, aware of a terrible responsibility.

Since 1916, except for an article on Grigoriev and a few lines of *Retribution*, he had written very little. His engrossing military duties, the communal life where people slept three or four to a room, didn't leave him any time. In Petersburg he was again a servant of the State, and his work for the Investigatory Commission was only the beginning of the work imposed on him. There was no question of his regaining that liberty, the sleepless nights and disordered days, which alone provided opportunities for writing. He did not complain. He knew that it was absolutely necessary to serve, in some way or another, the revolution he admired.

Two things seemed clear: there was a revolutionary people, strong and resolved to rise, ready to act. This people deserted, fraternized with the enemy, refused to obey Kerensky's orders, laughed at the Allies, laid siege to the trains and returned home. What did they matter, all the Milyukovs and their friends, Albert Thomas and the rest, who spoke of honour and duty!* This people had had enough, they didn't want to fight any more, they were tired. They wanted to share out the lands of the wealthy, occupy the factories, finish once and for all with the Church, palaces and banks. The second obvious thing was peace. It was becoming possible, even drawing close. That monstrous, horrible, useless, ugly, stupid thing, the war, could soon be over.

---

*P.N. Miluyukov (1859–1943), ex-Foreign Minister to the Provisional Government, interrogated by the Commission; Albert Thomas (1878–1932), French politician and Socialist member of the Chamber of Deputies 1910–21. – Trs.

XXI

Nothing was simple for Blok, even in those first months of the revolution. Small matters bothered him, things he couldn't avoid seeing and judging. In the Ukraine, Russian soldiers fraternized with the Germans, but in the north, on the Riga front, the Germans made gigantic advances. There was a bread shortage; rifle fire sounded in the night; in the distance, guns thundered. Was this the revolution 'without bloodshed'? Discontent increased. In the streets the cry went up: 'Let the Germans come quickly, otherwise we'll die of hunger!' At the front the death penalty was again imposed for desertion, and no one protested. Censorship was also reinstated. Finland proclaimed its independence and soon the Ukraine, in its turn, did the same. 'Great Russia' was certainly collapsing. Bolshevism was much discussed and two names – Lenin, Trotsky – caught Blok's attention. He was attracted by the doctrine that stirred the revolutionaries with whom he sympathized, while at the same time – like many others – he thought that it was all German-inspired propaganda.

A terrible drought devastated the land. The forests and fields around Petersburg burned. Heavy, dirty yellow smoke reached as far as the outskirts of the capital. There was no prospect of a harvest. Anguish and sadness weighed down the whole country. Blok was distraught: 'Now what? Has the revolution itself been lost?' he noted in July. 'Weariness, weariness! Everything is black... For Russia, as for me, there is no future.'

A choice had to be made. In July, Lenin and Trotsky attempted to seize power. Although they failed, it was felt that they didn't consider themselves beaten.

'I cannot choose. Every choice is an act of will. For that I have to look to the sky and the sky, today, is empty for me.

... I will not make a choice. There is nothing to be proud of; I don't understand anything!'

Everyone around him was making a choice. The intellectuals supported Kerensky, wanting the war to continue until Germany was defeated and also the immediate arrest of Lenin and Trotsky. Blok disapproved of these measures. He agreed with the people, but his agreement was not based on a considered and definite choice. He agreed with the people, yet he was still torn by doubts and contradictions, and obsessed by troubled thoughts. He clung to the feeling that he'd always had – repressed, hidden, born of mistrust – of aversion to the West. It was the feeling that was to inspire *The Scythians.*

> Today the great liars, French, English, Japanese, are even more of a threat to us than the Germans. We are tired of their threats. We are sick of it, but Europe does not want to understand, our weariness is too simple for their sly minds. Everyone distrusts us more than ever, they are mortally afraid of us because they know that we could, at a given moment, let through the flood of the yellow race which would invade not merely Reims cathedral but all their sacred shops. We are the lock. No one who knows these 'revolutionary forces' is forbidden to open the sluice gates.

Merezhkovsky tried to group around himself those who still had the strength and will to defend themselves against 'the coming shadows'. Blok tried to escape notice. People were already talking about his Bolshevism; he did not react. Life had become 'loathsome' again. Lyuba was far away, playing in Pskov, and he knew now that he could not live without her. 'Lyuba, Lyuba, Lyuba' he cried on every page of his diary. 'Lyuba, what will come of all this? Lyuba, where are you?' 'I pray God, I pray Lyuba.' And the same thought keeps recurring: 'It's time to be done with all of this.'

She came, but what could he give her now? Distraught, weary, ageing, a ray of sunshine made him smile sadly: 'There, a little warmth and light for me, poor beast!' Lyuba had her life, the theatre, her successes; he, at thirty-seven, complained of back pains and spoke of the approach of 'gentle old age'. His health was more and more of a worry; he had strange pains in the back and legs that the doctors could not pinpoint. He monitored his illness in a spirit of curiosity: 'Suddenly, for a few moments, an unbearable pain, driving one mad.' And two days later: 'Sometimes I think that I might go out of my mind.'

Lyuba was there but their life bored her and she did not hide it. The summer was dry and burning, full of violent storms; at midnight electricity was cut off and they had to go in search of candles. The newspapers were nervous, the people even more so. It was stifling. A muted, disquieting, oppressive anger weighed on the city and only needed a sign to break out. 'I don't know how to entertain Lyuba,' Blok wrote on 3 August; 'she likes to be with me, but I know that she finds it difficult to listen to my conversation.' And Lyuba, overcome by Blok's despair, proposed 'collective suicide'. 'Everything is too confused,' she said, 'too horrible; it will never be sorted out again.'

Women were still fascinated by him. Mlle Delmas came to see him; friends and strangers sent him letters and declarations of love. Every night the same shadowy woman waited opposite his window. But women no longer interested him, and if he went to the window it was to listen to the guns whose grumblings drew closer. The Kornilov riots were triggered off. Would he be able to live freely again one day, in peace and calm? Cease being a civil servant? Would the Investigatory Commission go on sitting much longer? Everything indicated that it would, and at the same time they were asking him to be part of a commission on the repertory of the former imperial theatres. He did not have the right to refuse, and found himself doubly tied to an organism already more bureaucratic than revolutionary.

'Mlle Delmas has sent Lyuba a letter and some flour; tomorrow is my birthday. My personal life is nothing but a series of humiliations. I notice it as soon as there is a lull in my work...'

And the war still went on! Everything was falling apart, impoverished, breaking down, drifting along. All that remained was to take walks in Shuvalovo Park and bathe in the lake. Sometimes, when he had a few hours free, he took the train and fled; he would spend the night drinking in the places he'd known well and to which he was always drawn when life weighed too heavily on him.

September. 'Everything and everyone is going to the dogs. People are becoming weaker. I have succumbed to the pressure of work and anxieties. No break in the clouds! Famine spreads, the cold already makes itself felt. And the war is not over.'

October. On Trotsky's orders armed workers take to the streets of Petersburg; Lenin gives an inflammatory, decisive speech. The cruiser *Aurora* comes up the river and trains its guns on the Winter Palace. Power passes into the hands of the Bolsheviks.

A glacial, heavy, black winter. At night the dark streets were empty. The prisons proved too small to contain the new prisoners, acclaimed only the day before. No more contact! They were separated not only from the rest of the world but from Russia itself. No news from Moscow! The front was in complete disarray; what did the alliances matter now? The Germans advanced and there was nothing to stop them.

A letter arrived from Shakhmatovo, a painful letter, written by an estate worker:

Your Excellency Gracious Lady Aleksandra Andreyevna – the estate has been sealed up; they took away the keys from me, they took the grain and left nothing but fifteen or eighteen poods of flour. The house was ransacked. Aleksandr Aleksandrovich's desk was broken open with an axe; they have rooted through everything. I cannot describe the horror and the vandalism. They broke down the library door. These are not free citizens, they are savages, wild beasts. From today, despite my own feelings, I'm leaving the Party. Curses on all these fools!

I sold the horse for 230 roubles. I'll leave soon. If you are coming, let me know first, because they require me to inform them of your arrival, but I don't want to be an informer and at the same time I'm afraid of their wrath. There are those who are sorry for you and those who hate you. Reply to this quickly.

They played on the piano, smoked, spat everywhere; they took Sir's caps, took the binoculars, the dagger, the knives, the medals, the money and I don't know what else, because I felt sick and went away…

Blok did not reply to the letter. He never went to Shakhmatovo again; in 1918 the house, with its books and archives, was destroyed by fire. One of Blok's cousins, passing by in 1920, could no longer recognize the place; the brambles had taken over.

Nevertheless, one had to live – that is to say, believe in something, love someone, long for, wait, hope for some kind of joy. But hatred impregnated the soul. Hatred for all those who expected nothing and did nothing; for the bourgeoisie in all its manifestations, strong in its accumulated material and spiritual values; hatred for Merezhkovsky and Sologub who wanted to 'keep their hands clean'; hatred for the young lady who sang stupid songs behind the partition, waiting for a 'stallion' to come to her; hatred for the revolutionary socialists of the Left, whom Blok had joined and who, hand in glove with the Bolsheviks, quibbled over a peace settlement; hatred even for Gorky's paper because it criticized Trotsky's line. He wanted to block his ears against the echoes of the distractions of the drunken crowd who smashed and raided shops, pillaged wine stores and became disgustingly drunk. 'O my dear, my beloved rabble!' Blok didn't want to hear any more talk of all the useless, stupid decrees which didn't succeed in shoring up the little 'revolutionary order' that remained; or to know anything about the clauses of the Brest-Litovsk Treaty, which everyone around him was busy criticizing.

For Blok who, since 1907, had explored in a series of articles the relationship between the intellectuals and the people, one thing was plain: for a hundred years the intelligentsia had desired political change in Russia, the fall of tsarism and the advent of a new class, so they simply had to accept the October revolution, without judgement or reserve; they had to recognize it and support it. This is what he wrote in the last of his articles, 'The Intelligentsia and the Revolution', at the end of that crowded, cruel year of 1917. At the moment the abhorred war was ending, at the moment in which 'the dictatorship of the proletariat' was at last revealing to him 'the true face of the people', he expressed for the first and only time his feelings about the October revolution, to which he said he was totally committed. This article, and *The Twelve*, which he wrote a month later, were the essence of Blok's revolutionary work.

'What is war?' he asks in 'The Intelligentsia and the Revolution'.

> It is mud, blood and boredom. It is hard to say which is the more sickening: blood flowing or boredom reigning. Yet this is called 'the Great War', the 'war for the liberation of oppressed peoples'. No, people are not liberated like this!
>
> If the intelligentsia loved the indications of revolution, today they must rejoice: we loved dissonance, various melodies in the orchestra, but if we *really* loved them, and not just because they were a pleasant titillation of our nerves in an elegant theatre after a good dinner, we must listen to them and love them now, these sounds which are resounding in the orchestra of the world. And in listening we must remember that it is the same music, speaking of the same things.

He foresaw a tragic end for those who endured the upheavals. 'But those of us who survive will become the masters of incalculable spiritual values.'

'We are the links in a single chain; we are responsible for the past. The sins of our fathers weigh on us. If everyone does not feel this, the best must feel it.'

The intelligentsia must flee from everything 'bourgeois', forget themselves and not weep for their dead – whether people or ideas. 'Listen to the great music of the future; the air is full of it. Do not look for false or inharmonious notes in the grand melody of that orchestra.'

'Sentimentality must not put obstacles in the way of the spirit. The beautiful is infinitely difficult... With your whole body, with your whole soul, with your whole conscience, listen to the revolution!'

Bely was sometimes in Petersburg, sometimes who knew where. Esenin was there, sentimental as a schoolboy, his ideas muddled but his talent indisputable; the rest remained in the shadows. It was said that things were different in Moscow, that Bryusov and the Futurists were all in agreement with the new government. But Moscow was so far away! Here, Sologub and others talked of sabotaging the government.

Blok forced himself to listen to 'this music of the revolution'; he was haunted by it. Everything else had faded away: the infamy of life, mediocrity, stupidity; night and day he listened. And, without his knowing, an image detached itself from the shadows and imposed its presence. With horror, disgust, alarm – not with bliss, calm and serenity – he recognized it: it was the image of Christ. 'Sometimes I profoundly hate this effeminate image.' But he could not turn away from it. 'If you look carefully at the whirling snowflakes, along this road, you will see Jesus appear.' The obsession grew: 'Christ is at their head, indisputably. The question is not whether they are worthy of Him. What is terrible is that He is there, once again, and that there was nobody else until now. The Other?'

And he wrote *The Twelve*. This poem has nothing to do with imaginary incidents. They marched just like this across Petersburg during the winter of 1918, day and night in the cold and snow, smashing, killing, raping, shouting their liberation songs, guns over their shoulders. One saw them in the little streets around Pryazhka, on Nevsky Prospekt, in the Summer Gardens, on the quays now littered with broken glass and stones. And in front of the 'Twelve', as real as they were, Blok saw this 'effeminate ghost'. He didn't understand what it meant. He closed his eyes, but it would not go away.

The 'Right' spoke of blasphemy and hated him ferocious-ly. The 'Left' – Lunacharsky, Kamenev* – did not view this 'outdated symbol' favourably. Kamenev said to him: 'You shouldn't read these lines out loud because you are sancti-fying in them what we others, old socialists, most dread.' And Trotsky advised him to replace Christ with Lenin.

The Twelve became Blok's breadwinner. Every night Lyuba recited the poem in an artists' cabaret, where poets, the trendy bourgeois, odd types and heavily made-up women, went to hear 'the wife of the famous Blok who has sold himself to the Bolsheviks'. Lyuba earned money, and there was no question of theatre work at the time.

The Scythians, which appeared just as the Brest-Litovsk Treaty was signed, seemed to be a commentary on the Treaty addressed to the Allies. For Russia the war was over and, full of hope, Blok invited Europe to make a choice. If not... And these were not idle threats. From the depths of Petersburg, half dead, Blok threatened the 'Paestums' of Europe,[†] but he himself did not realize that the poem was a *de profundis*.

Once again Vladimir Solovev made an appearance. The epigraph to *The Scythians* was his:

> Panmongolism! The word is strange
> But it falls caressingly on my ear.

It was the Mongols, that is the Eurasian Russians, who spoke. Asia had been wounded by Europe; for centuries she had been aware of being ugly, dirty, poor, ignorant. Europe was beautiful, clean, prosperous, cultivated. But in Asia 'the names are legion' and it was this multitude that would bring about the demise of its rival. How to respond to the West's

---

*A.V. Lunacharsky (1875–1933), first Bolshevik Commissar for Education; A.P. Kamensky (1876–1963), poet and dramatist. – Trs

†In *The Scythians*, Blok writes: 'The day may follow whose sun rising brings / no shadow where your Paestums stood' – that is the Scythians threaten to erase the ruins of the West. – Trs

disdain? How could the 'Yellow Men' avenge themselves on the 'White'?

Everything that Russia had suppressed over the centuries rises up from these lines full of bitterness and rage. Unrequited love for Europe, envy, a longing – which had never found any echo – to be united with her, all this was transformed into implacable hatred. The jealousy of Peter the Great, of Pushkin and of Herzen shows through *The Scythians*.

Blok was very aware of the ultimate weapon at Russia's disposal: to allow passage for the Asiatic hordes to surge into Europe. It would be the path of hatred.

But what would she do with her love of the West? The 'Yellow' wanted to be the brother of the 'White'; love oppressed her, she succumbed to its weight. This excessive love, inconceivable to a European, is terrible; it leads to the ruin of the lover and the beloved. And the Russian wept in offering to Europe an eternal peace in which he himself did not believe.

The Scythians does not have Blok's individual magic. It is significant rather than beautiful. Its polemical character makes it an imperfect work which can be appreciated but not really loved.

The Twelve appears as the first product of the revolution. An undeniable genius marks this poem, which opens the way to the poetry of Mayakovsky and all future revolutionary poetry. With extraordinary virtuosity Blok uses the songs and sayings of the street, and this confers a unique quality on *The Twelve*. In the way that Lermontov, with his poem 'The Song of Tsar Ivan Vasilivich, of his young *oprichnik* and of the gallant merchant Kalachnikov' had revived the Russian folklore of the *bylinas*, an epic literary genre, Blok immortalized revolutionary folklore in *The Twelve*.

In *The Scythians*, he tried to speak in the name of the Russian people. Perhaps, in *The Twelve*, he wanted to write his poem *for* the people? It is clear that he wanted to write in a totally new way, to make something that was not only beautiful but useful. Everything in him and around him had been shattered by these events, and this poem (which, moreover, is much more dated than more 'Symbolist' poems by Blok) exactly reflects the state of the poet's soul and the image of the city – an unforgettable image – in that first winter of a new era.

XXII

Universal brotherhood! Eternal peace! The abolition of money! Equality, employment. The beautiful, the marvellous *Internationale*! The world is your country. No longer any ownership. If you have two coats, one is taken from you for someone who has none. You can keep one pair of shoes, and if you need a box of matches, the 'Match Centre' will provide one. The same petrol ration for an Academician, a new baby, a worker, a prostitute. At the end of six months the State has nothing, the people have nothing, nobody has anything, the starving country goes barefoot. The young march enthusiastically, proud before that old Europe which is still trying desperately to beat the Germans. They sing exhilarating choruses, recite poems, with empty stomachs and shining eyes. The children have never seen an orange, don't know whether Nicholas II lived before or after Alexander II, or that there used to be several classes of train travel...

Crossing the ghost town one encounters an extraordinary and fascinating life. Everyone is ghostlike, weighing nothing. The old die; the rebels are shot; those who do not wish to understand that the earthly paradise is close at hand flee to the borders. In the winter ice, in the transparent summer light, the capital, like a great invalid, begins to change its appearance.

But the theatres are packed. *Don Carlos*, *Turandot*, *Les Fourberies de Scapin* are performed two hundred, four hundred, eight hundred times. Poems by Blok, by Sologub, by Akhmatova, by Gumilev are printed on wrapping paper; as are works by as yet unknown young poets, who sing the heroes of the civil war, the lack of bread, love – anything and everything, since no one asks anything of them and they ask nothing of anyone.

125

No one knows for sure what is going on elsewhere. It is said that Siberia and south Russia have been invaded by the enemies of the new regime, that in Moscow there are extraordinary things happening in the theatre and the literary world. But no one knows exactly what! They don't even know whether Vyacheslav Ivanov is still alive and whether Bryusov is still writing. All that is so far away!

In Petersburg Gorky was now in charge and created institutions that would raise the cultural level of the masses. In quick succession came the publishing house World Literature – for translations of world masterpieces – and Proletkult, the proletarian school of culture where the young worker poets came to listen to advice from poets of the old regime. Special courses were set up to explain to museum guides the relationship between the paintings of Fra Angelico and feudalism. In the theatres there were commentaries on Marx for the director, the actress, the sweeper and the prompt. Grass pushed up through the pavements and the marble of the palaces lost its shine; there were no cabs or trams. Petersburg, like Venice, resounded with footsteps.

Blok was employed not only on the Commission for the Reorganization of Theatres and Spectacles – where, under the direction of Madame Kameneva, he was assembling the new repertoire – but also on the publishing panel of the People's Commissariat for Education. The Extraordinary Investigatory Commission into unlawful acts by former ministers was wound up, but other bodies sprang up and required his presence. Some days he was at as many as five sittings. And there was still the 'Scythian' group, the rump of the old Left revolutionary socialists, to which he was committed. He was permanently 'mobilized'!

Two documents, written at about the same time, give us some insight into Blok's state of mind. The first was a response to Sologub's enquiry: 'What is the role of the Russian poet today?' Blok responded to the question as a poet; he had nothing to say about food supplies, vacant thrones, parliamentarianism or religious processions. What did the poet have to do at present?

> A poet must realize that Russia as she was no longer exists, and will never return. Russia and Europe will still exist, but they will be different, and probably life will be ten times more terrible. But everything will be different; that which is dead cannot be revived. A new era is opening for the world. The old civilization, the old social ideas, the old religion are dead. They tried to return to life, but they had lost their vitality, and we who are witness to their death-throes, to their last, agonized convulsions, may well be required to watch their decomposition with our utmost strength. Do not forget that Rome lived on for five hundred years after the birth of Christ, but could only decay and rot away; it was already no more than a corpse. A poet must be inflamed by a holy anger against all those who wish to reinvigorate such a corpse. But this anger must not degenerate into hatred – hatred is a temptation – and thus the poet must never forget the truth that ours is a great epoch, and that all hatred is unworthy of it. But one must never lose sight of *social inequality*. This idea must not be weakened by 'humanism', political economy, sentimentality. The constant thought of social inequality is an elevated and a wrathful thought.
>
> A poet must prepare for the even greater events still to come, and he must know how to bow before them.

The second document is a farewell letter to Madame Gippius who, together with Merezhkovsky, was leaving for Paris.

> I am writing to you in prose because I want to say more to you than you have said to me, and not just lyrical things.* I address myself to your humanity, to your intelligence, to your loyalty, to your sensitivity, because I do not wish to hurt you, nor to upset you as you have upset me. That is why I do not address myself to that 'mortal innocence' of which there is even more in you than there is in me.

*She had dedicated a poem to him.

There is 'fateful emptiness' in me, as there is in you. If this is something very serious, we cannot reproach each other. Others will judge us. If it is nothing more than a 'private' thing, due to our 'decadence', it is not worth talking about in the face of present events. I should like to remind you of something that concerns us both: it was not 1917 that divided us but 1905, when as yet I understood and knew so little. Our best encounters took place during the years of reaction, when the principal thing slumbered within us but only the secondary effects were visible. I have not changed – that is my tragedy and also yours – but alongside the secondary effects the principal has awakened within me. In our relationship there has always been something obscure, the knot was always too tight. It was natural, perhaps, but painful. Everything was painful during those years; the knots were too tight, they could only be cut.

The great October cut them. That is not to say that life will not make other knots. It has done so already, but they will be different.

I do not know (or perhaps I know only too well) why you did not see the greatness of October behind its grimaces – there weren't very many of them, and they might have been worse. Thus you do not know that 'Russia will be no more' as Rome is no more, not just since the fifth century but since the first. That England, France and Germany will be no more! That the old world is at melting-point! That the new is coming into being!

1919. Amid the cold and hunger, life was beginning to be regulated. Everyone had to have a job, belong to some organization, be in the service of the State. To stay at home meant to have no rations. Anyway Blok never refused to 'mobilize', and every night there were gatherings, lectures, obligatory meetings. His relations with people were confined to work. He had to choose classic plays, read and prepare accounts of modern plays, explain the chosen works to artists, discuss propaganda plays with the directors of 'People's Theatres', attend rehearsals and performances. The plans were wide-ranging but few of them were realized. Madame Kameneva and Madame Andreyeva, Gorky's wife, who also worked on the Theatre Commission, were at loggerheads. Madame Andreyeva tore Blok away from her rival and named him director of the Bolshoi Dramatichesky Theatre. He had a great deal to do but little freedom, as the theatre's political commissar and Madame Andreyeva had the right of veto. Nevertheless he went about his duties conscientiously and, at the beginning, with a degree of enthusiasm. The theatre's repertoire was essentially classical: Shakespeare, Molière, Schiller, Merezhkovsky's historical plays, Goldoni's comedies. Blok had to make speeches, plan the year's programme with his committee, go over new translations. They put on *Les Brigands, Othello, The Blue Bird* and, as it was then called, the ex-*King Lear*. The arts were not yet under terrible pressure from social controls, and in the early years there was considerable freedom in this field. The artists of the Bolshoi, getting on in years and cultured, were proud and happy to be working with Blok. But he couldn't devote all his time to the theatre, despite the pleasure it gave him; he had other demands on his time, above all those of 'World Literature'.

Gorky, who wanted the masterpieces of world literature translated into Russian, had mobilized all the 'cultural forces' for this massive task. Old translations were unearthed and reworked; those by Grandmother Beketov and Madame Kublitskaya were reissued, revised by Blok, which meant that he could obtain a little tobacco on the black market. Although there had been talk of abolishing money, the State still paid for work in hundreds of thousands and even millions of roubles. There was no more wine, only illicitly distilled vodka. In the World Literature offices, where Academicians, teachers, poets, writers and those without any profession came looking for work, they gathered round Gorky several times a week and drank sugarless 'tea', a weak infusion of dried carrots, which was often the only hot drink they would have all day. Worn-out and threadbare clothing became more and more basic and ill-assorted; often people wore neither shirt nor waistcoat beneath their coats; nothing more than a garment made out of an old blanket. Blok obstinately remained clean-shaven, kept his white polo-neck sweater clean, and never spoke of his privations.

And it was indeed a hard life. For months the thermometer showed minus 20°. Each day he had to carry heavy logs up from the cellar, walk three hours coming and going between the Pryazhka and the centre of town, and swallow the same barley or millet *kasha* without butter or oil, often even without salt. Rations were meagre: 150 grams of damp bread full of bran, a bit of dried fish as hard as stone, a few herrings, sometimes a little lard and tobacco. Blok sold his books, his furniture and such precious things as he still had. Exhausted by this life, thin, sad, silent, he fought with all his might against giving way, giving in, falling ill. He gave a series of lectures on Heine, whom he translated for World Literature, and agreed to collaborate on 'Scenes from History' – another of Gorky's ideas to raise the cultural level of the masses. It involved writing a series of historical scenes on a set subject, to be performed in the popular theatres. Blok's contribution, *Rameses*, was about Egypt.

He published *The Grey Morning*, a collection of poems written between 1907 and 1916 but not included in the *Third Volume*, and a collection of his youthful poems. As they brought in money, he published everything he could find, articles, plays...

Weary after two years of poverty and isolation in an over-crowded Moscow apartment, Bely arrived in Petersburg in the hope of finding life there a little easier. His wife remained abroad. Unhappy, exhausted, hungry, he looked for a corner to curl up in, a bit of warmth and food. But he wasn't made to live among wolves, he could never manage on his own and didn't know how to go about getting extra rations. In an ice-cold room, motionless, huddled beneath his overcoat, he gave in to despair. The ink froze in the inkwell so that he couldn't write; he concentrated on patching his only pair of trousers and, to avoid typhus, battled continually against fleas.

'Perpetual death,' he wrote to his wife (in an unpublished letter) in 1921, when he had left Russia, 'death staring us in the face; and that feeling, in 1919, in 1920, when the first snowflakes began to fall: they would cover us, they would bury us, they would conceal us from the rest of the world. This vast country was nothing more than a country condemned, an island cut off for ever from what we held dear.'

From Bely and Blok's meetings came the idea of a Free Philosophical Association. Blok inaugurated it by reading his paper on 'The Collapse of Humanism'; religious, philosophical and artistic questions were debated but the Association was short-lived. It was viewed suspiciously from the outset; in February 1919 its members were arrested, then released; surveillance became stricter and eventually the Association was deemed not to conform to Marxist ideas and was closed down for good in 1921.

Associations, groups, unions, committees came and went in swift succession, with Blok figuring as president, vice-president, honorary member. Despite the unease he felt among the Acmeists, among the young people who were complete strangers to him, he could not refuse to preside over the 'Poets' Union'. But after some discussion he was delighted to yield his place to Gumilev who, strongly influential among the young poets, assumed an authority and confidence that caused a number of clashes not only with Blok but also with the leaders and with Gorky at World Literature. Bely and friends of the 'Scythian' group proposed founding a journal and suggested that Blok be the editor. He agreed, and for two years he was one of the editors of *Zapiski Mechtateley* (Dreamers' Notes), the last of the free journals, proscribed in 1921.

Two clubs, the House of Arts and the Writers' House, were set up in Petersburg, and thus all the institutions concerned with art and with literature were centralized.

'Communes' were formed within the houses by painters and writers; schools of poetry, translation and literary history were set up. There were libraries, work rooms, meeting rooms and even canteens, where the inevitable *kasha* was served. And Blok, a council member of both houses, had to give up a bit more of his time!

Apartments were requisitioned and rooms were dealt out per person, often per couple. After the death of General Kublitsky in January 1920, Blok moved into the flat shared by his mother and his aunt, in the same block but two storeys lower down. It was easier to bring up the firewood, but relations between Lyuba and her mother-in-law were increasingly stormy; there were frequent scenes which pained Blok a great deal. The public of the arts cabaret had got tired of hearing *The Twelve*, and Lyuba had to take an engagement at the People's Theatre.

This young woman, used to being free and pampered, adapted uncomplainingly to her difficult, wearisome life: housework, cooking, washing, shopping, daily performances at the other end of town, returning on foot at night; hunger and cold did not break her spirit. She sold or bartered what she could lay hands on for frozen potatoes. A knapsack on her back, she returned from the theatre co-operative carrying her flour, salt and paraffin. There was no electricity any more, no phones, no other means of communication. All the horses had been eaten and it was only with an enormous amount of trouble, after many attempts and a lengthy search, that they could find one to take General Kublitsky's body to the cemetery. This exhausting, brutal life for Lyuba was another cause of Blok's suffering. He even sold his books to get a bit of money. He helped her as much as he could. In the cold dark night, the wind whipping his face, he made the long trek to the co-operative, dragging a child's sled. Along the frozen, deserted canal, across the dark city, in the thick, hard-packed snow, he walked with difficulty. Empty shops, broken windows, houses open to the winds, their doors long since ripped off and burnt, courtyards which the bursting of frozen pipes had filled with excrement: this was his path across the dead city.

> When you've been hounded, broken down
> by people, worries, emptiness
> when everything has come to dust
> that held your heart; when through the town
> – the municipal waste – you go
> home, giving out and giving up,
> and the hoar-frost has soldered up
> your lashes, as the winter glows,
> then for a moment, stop, and listen
> to the quiet of the night,
> and you will hear another life
> the rumour of the day had hidden;
> with new eyes you can see the smoke
> of watchfires, roadways thick with snow in
> the night that quietly waits for morning
> above the feather-bedded park
> whose sky is just another tome;
> you'll find within your scoured soul
> your mother's loving presence, while
> in that incomparable moment,
> the tracery on the streetlamp's glass,
> the frost that snagged and snarled your blood,
> the chilly distance of your love
> will light up in your grateful breast;
> to all of this you'll give your
> blessing, finding life so much more grand
> than the *quantum satis* of Ibsen's Brand:
> the world is beautiful, as ever.

This fragment is taken from the third section of *Retribution*, the poem which Blok couldn't finish for lack of time. He thought about it, at night, crossing the town; but as soon as he got home he was overwhelmed by worries. Sometimes it was the tax people, quibbling over procedure, sometimes the 'Building Committee' who wanted to turn him out one day, for no reason. Then there was the absurd obligatory night duty, shared with the other tenants, to mount guard in the street and courtyard. And on top of it all, no candles, no paraffin, no light.

In his stepfather's old room, behind a screen, he installed his bed, his writing-table, what was left of his library after selling or trading books for food; in the middle of the room, near the cast-iron stove, was the dining-table. There was nothing to be seen from the windows: no factory chimneys, no boats, no masts, no clouds. On free evenings Lyuba mended old clothes, Blok read and corrected playscripts for soldiers of the Red Army, sent to the Repertory Committee. And often he went to the theatre very early in the morning, not to sit on some committee but along with the actors and workers to tidy away the wood Madame Andreyeva had managed to get for heating.

XXIII

Spring arrived, and in the clarity of the white nights the city was revealed, its trees cut down, its houses collapsing, the grass already invading its broad streets. The palaces were empty, their bronze railings torn away; the embassies were abandoned and the ministries evacuated to Moscow. Death enveloped everything, majestic and beautiful. At sunrise people emerged, dignified in their tattered clothing and shoes without soles – carnival costumes – wretched but never ridiculous. Men with long hair, their coats billowing round their thin bodies, their faces half-starved and glowing, books under their arms, went to and fro like shadows between the Hermitage and the Academy, between the House of Art and the Free Philosophical Association. Some of them, like Gumilev, wore tails in the evening because they had no other garments. Pyast wore checked trousers, perhaps bought by his father at the World Fair in Paris; Chileiko, the Egyptologist, who was forty-five and looked sixty-five, never took off his overcoat, even when it was really hot; and Volinsky, the Italian Renaissance expert, slept with his galoshes on for fear they might be stolen. Nothing disturbed the grandeur of these places, of these shadowy figures, and the hungry young people who followed them – to the university halls, to the Hermitage, to concerts, in the streets – were equally worthy of this era.

The war between Acmeism and Symbolism had already lasted ten years, and Gumilev and Blok were still at loggerheads; Blok despised the airs put on by the leader of the Acmeists and his affectations copied from Bryusov. Gumilev played at being the Master, and haughtily demanded of the young – not very much younger than himself – respect rather than affection. Despite these faults, he had a noble and brave character.

'Blok is the best of men,' he used to say, 'not only the best of Russian poets, but the best of all those I've ever known. A pure soul, a loyal soul!... It's just that he doesn't understand anything about poetry.'

Blok did not dislike Gumilev personally; he admired his talent but was irritated by the Acmeist entourage. He hated the evenings organized by the Poets' Union where, in religious silence, they read poems, discussed the merits of form and solemnly attended to the 'Master', who assumed the role of judge. For Blok all this 'stank of Heredia', and one of his last articles was directed against these very same theories which left no room for inspiration. The article was never published because the proofs of the journal in which it was to appear were destroyed by police order: purely literary polemics were no longer desirable.

Anna Akhmatova, who had left the Acmeists in 1914 – she had been one of their glories – is the most extraordinary of all the shadowy women of Petersburg; her adversities and the vast multi-coloured shawl which enveloped her are legendary. She passed

> By the houses where in other days
> We danced and drank champagne

and wrote poems of Petersburg in distress – Petersburg, the city of poets! After all, Sologub was there, and Bely and Khodasevich had arrived from Moscow, and Kuzmin, almost as wretched as Pyast, with his large eyes, stubbled cheeks and his bag always on his back. But the 'sacred friendship of poets' of which Pushkin had spoken had been warped.

> We are each other's secret enemies
> We are strangers, deaf and jealous.

Since 1905 Blok had had no poetic rival. He had never felt jealous or hated anyone, but neither had he been keen to have friends. And now he felt less keen than ever. There were too many people around this 'trooper', too many people he had to talk to. And inside himself he was so troubled, so sad, so despairing. The confessions in his diary are few and discreet in the year 1920; frequent searches made writing dangerous and encouraged caution. However certain collected jottings are significant:

> Art is incompatible with pressure exercised by any power whatsoever. (January 1920)

> I have become so bad that yesterday I did a terrible thing. A little boy skated into my path on the pavement. I pushed him and he fell over. I'm ashamed. May God forgive me! (January 1921)

> In the depth of my despair, piercing early morning thoughts. I must learn how to declaim *The Twelve*, become a poet-balladeer. Then we could get money and all sorts of good things. (January 1921)

> My next collection of poems will be called 'Black Days'. (February 1921)

> The louse has taken over the world: it's a fact. And now every-thing is going to change, but not in the way we'd hoped, not in the way we would like and for which we have lived – in another way entirely. (April 1921)

In his personal notebooks the jottings are even more urgent:

> There is no way out of it all! Leave everything, sell everything, go far away, into the sun! Live differently!

> Such sadness! When will it all be over? It is time to wake up!

His aunt, who was his official biographer, glides over these last years but even she states that he worked 'because he could not do otherwise', that 'all the fires were out', that he was 'profoundly disillusioned', that 'around him every-thing was grey and dismal, and he was locked away in his sadness'.

Everything wearied him, everything seemed futile, but the most tedious of his duties were still the innumerable committee meetings, where everyone spoke for hours and where he also had to speak – and nothing came of them. The two literary evenings he held, one on the occasion of his lecture to mark the twentieth anniversary of Solovev's death, the other when he read the first two sections of *Retribution*, brought him no pleasure.

To leave! The words, at first mentioned casually, now constantly cropped up in conversation. The idea of departure recurred with increasing force, and Blok realized with dread that he himself was becoming interested in the possibility. Where to go? How to leave? To go away for ever? Or just for a while, so that one could eat, sleep, forget the cold and privations and terrors and take hold of oneself again? Akhmatova had decided to stay. Gumilev said nothing; his private life was shrouded in mystery. Sologub hoped to leave for good, and although they hadn't declared themselves, Bely and Remizov had been trying to get passports for several months. Even Gorky, with the help of his doctor, was trying to get a German visa. Blok didn't think of emigrating, but he dreamed of a long rest in Finland. He waited, hesitated, then decided to put in a request.

In the hermetically sealed city, obsessive dreams were born. As in a fairy-tale, but one which might perhaps come true, people thought about Europe, which still existed and where the war was over, where one could live, write, even sweep the streets.

The occasional train began to run, and it was suggested to Blok that he organize a series of lectures and literary evenings in Moscow. In April 1920 he went off, secretly hoping to see Stanislavsky and re-open the question of *The Rose and the Cross*. As in 1904, on his first trip, Moscow acclaimed him. But it was no longer to a restricted, closed circle of intellectuals that he spoke now. Two thousand people, jammed into a hall packed to bursting every night, listened to him, applauded him, astonished by the music of his poetry, overwhelmed by its tragic lucidity. A crowd waited for him at the end, hailed him and accompanied him; the memory of these 'Blok days' lingered for a long time.

'How handsome the Muscovites are!'

There too they were cold and hungry, but the presence in the Kremlin of Lenin, of Trotsky, of Kamenev, and the feverish political life gave an extraordinary bustle to the city. Moscow, swarming and overcrowded, with new people arriving every day, now reflected the new Russia. Bryusov had joined the Communist Party; Vyacheslav Ivanov, nowhere to be seen, was preparing for departure. The former poets were absent; the Futurists, with Bobrov and Mayakovsky, were triumphant, and put their poetry and their energies in the service of propaganda. At the Kremlin, the Kamenevs received Blok coldly. If he was admired for his past, people knew that nothing could be expected of him in the future. For the first time he heard the now very fashionable expression: to use people, to squeeze them like lemons! For the Kremlin, Blok was a man who had been used. This was roughly the opinion expressed by Bobrov at a meeting and in his presence:

'Blok is dead. Blok no longer exists. What are his books? A fatal boredom, an unspeakable horror emanates from them. Pages full of prayers in the void. His decay spreads over everything. Blok has signed his own verdict. He no longer exists!'

But the enthusiastic crowd which accompanied him to the station, pressing round him and tossing flowers, did not share that opinion. 'Come back!' they shouted. 'We love you! You belong to us!'

After the bubbling, noisy life of Moscow, the anguished calm and silence of Petersburg, its mutilated beauty, made a painful impression on Blok. He brought back a little money, but no hope of seeing his play performed. Several theatres were interested in it but all said the same: Wait and see what happens.

XXIV

The first serious signs of the illness that was to carry him off dated from 1918. He had back pains, and his heart suffered strain when he carried up the wood. From 1919, in letters to close friends, he spoke of scurvy and boils, then of breathlessness which he put down to heart trouble, but which had a deeper cause than his physical state. He complained of deafness, yet he could obviously hear; it was a different deafness he spoke of, one that prevented his hearing the music he had heard all his life, that music which, in 1918, allowed him to go on writing poems. 'The air is mute; everything is becoming terribly silent.'

'I have no more air to breathe, I stifle. If I should become ill…?'

His relations with people were difficult and his home was sad. He didn't go to bed at night but remained sitting in an armchair, neglecting his duties; in the daytime he wandered round the apartment and in the streets, bravely struggling against his illness. The final year was appalling: everything seen, everything understood, no illusions remaining. It was the third year of retribution.

'I no longer have a body or a soul. I am sick as never before. The fever never lessens and everything makes me ill. So I can no longer say: We keep fit to this day. Dear, dirty, grunting little mother Russia has swallowed me, like a sow her piglet.'

And this exchange with a friend who criticized his 1918 poems is painfully clear:

— Ah! You had faith, you were indulgent! I envy you. You said: 'Everything old has been sent to the devil!' And Russia?
— Russia is no longer.
— So why have you written these verses about Russia?

– I was bidding her farewell.

And for yet another winter, that of 1920–21, he once again had to carry up wood from the cellar and attend wordy meetings every day, which certainly had no effect. There was no paper for publications, no scenery or costumes for the theatres. Cultural matters were increasingly controlled by limited, mediocre minds, often overtly leading that terrible campaign which had already found a name: 'the campaign for the degradation of culture' (the phrase used originally by the head of the movement, Levidov).

His state worsened and the doctors mentioned arteriosclerosis, but Blok's morale was so low that it sometimes seemed that he was dying not of his illness but of distress. He had to get away. Lyuba approached everyone, but in vain; everything took so long!

In February 1921 Blok took part in an evening organized to mark the anniversary of Pushkin's death, an evening which had to be repeated three times as the hall at the the Writers' House wasn't large enough to accommodate the public. When his name was called he rose, thin, his face flushed, his hair greying, his glance heavy and lifeless; he wore as always his white sweater, a black jacket, felt boots. Hands in his pockets, he spoke. Among the public there were those who felt as he did, but others had come along to seize on what what hidden behind his words; there were representatives from the government, from the police, and the young people who would soon build a new era. Blok spoke:

> Through the ages bureaucrats have been the dregs of the State. But they should take care, because we can also call them by another name if they start to force poetry down certain roads, conspiring against its secret freedom, opposed to what has been its own destiny to accomplish...
>
> Pushkin is dead but, as Schiller said, 'it is not for little boys that the *Poza* die.' Pushkin was not killed by d'Anthès alone! It was lack of air that killed him. And his era died with him.
>
> 'It's time, my friend, it's time! The heart begs for peace...'

this was the farewell sigh of Pushkin and also of his era. 'There is no happiness in this world, but there is peace and freedom …'* Peace! Freedom! For every poet they are indispensable. And behold how peace and freedom are taken from us; not our calm little lives, but the peace of the soul necessary to all creation. Not the freedom to speak, to utter words, but the freedom to create, the secret freedom. And thus the poet dies, because he can no longer breathe: life, for him, has lost its direction.

We are dying, but art will remain.

Thus spoke Blok six months before he died, and those who were listening were witness not only to a brilliant lecture on literature but also to a terrible drama, played out before their very eyes. A month later, at the Bolshoi Dramatichesky Theatre, he appeared at an evening of poetry. Everything that hovered behind the magic of his poems subdued the audience; as they listened, they felt a pang of anguish; they cheered him, a wave of love and enthusiasm rose up towards him. Few poets have known such a triumph.

His face impassive, looking up beyond the highest tiers, Blok read in a monotone. They asked for poems about Russia. 'But all these are about Russia,' he replied.

His face was severely beautiful:

> I myself am not the man I once was –
> Inaccessible, baleful, pure and proud.

He recited 'To the Muse', *On the Field of Kulikovo*, poems from *The Beautiful Lady*. But he seemed to forget *The Twelve*, and when people called out for it, a painful twitching changed his expression.

His illness grew, and the doctors knew perfectly well the origin of the mental suffering against which Blok fought so desperately. 'I'm becoming deaf,' he kept saying. He no longer heard 'the music of the revolution', he no longer heard any music. Another might have said, 'I no longer

*The quotations are from one of Pushkin's last poems.

appreciate beauty, I've lost all faith.'

In May 1921 he went to Moscow for the last time, but he was very ill, finding it hard to walk and breathe; he was very pleased to obtain, after numerous requests, authorization for a taxi to the station. He saw few people, the literary evenings exhausted him. His leg was giving him trouble and he could no longer walk without a stick. His fingers were bandaged. One day, re-reading his poem 'The Corpse among Men' he said:'That's my situation, but I didn't know it!'

Nothing seemed to touch him any more; he was indifferent to the world and one had the impression that he was asleep. One day he was found dozing on a bench in the avenue; another time, his face grey, his eyes dead, unrecognizable, he was immobilized in the middle of the room. It was difficult to wake him from this sleepwalking.

On his return from Moscow he retired to his room for good. His pains became unbearable; he couldn't sleep; he choked when lying down. In periods of remission his long fine hands flicked through the pages of *Retribution*, which he was correcting and wanted to finish. And during this spring he wrote his last pages of prose, 'Neither dream nor reality'.

> The peasants who sang so well in chorus brought back syphilis from Moscow and infected the whole village. The merchant who owned the field became an alcoholic and, in a drunken stupor, set fire to the hay on his estate. The deacon had bastards. The roof of Fyodor's *isba* fell in, but Fyodor didn't think of repairing it. At our house the old began to die and the young to age. My uncle started to say stupid things, which he never had before. As for me, I went out one morning to cut down the lilac.
>
> The lilac bush was noble, a hundred years old... I cut it down altogether. Afterwards it was the turn of the silver-birch grove. I cut it down. Then there was a gully. From the gully I could see nothing except my own house overhead. It is now open to all the winds, to all the storms. If I dig, it will fall in and bury me...

One day, wishing to flee from his soul, he went for a walk down the calmest, cleanest streets. But his soul followed him. It was hard for it to follow him because it was weary, whereas he had a youthful step. Suddenly, above the roof of a tall house, in the grey dusk of a winter's day, a face appeared. She stretched her hands towards him and said

— I have been striving to reach you for a long time, from the pure, silent regions of the sky. The poisonous smoke of the city gives me a dirty cloak. The telegraph wires cut across my arms. Stop always calling me by different names! I have only one. Stop looking for me here and there! I am right in front of you.

The terrible pain did not let up. Visits were forbidden. The end was near.

This summer of 1921 was marked as a black page in Russian poetry; those who lived through it would never forget it. Sologub, who was waiting for his visa to go abroad, was ordered to stay. In desperation his wife threw herself into the Neva, from which her husband recovered her body the next spring.

Gorky departed. Remizov and his wife, having finally got all their papers in order, also departed. Bely was promised a passport. Gumilev, arrested on 3 August, was shot at the end of the month. Suddenly there was the sense of living at the edge of an abyss, into which, with incredible speed, everything that was beautiful, great, dear, irreplaceable was disappearing. With extraordinary intensity one lived though what was perceived to be the end of an era. And this spectacle had a grandiose horror, a poignant sadness, heavy with meaning.

The last days of Blok's illness were excruciating; he cried out night and day. Without having regained consciousness, he died on 7 August 1921. That evening, his passport arrived.

There were no newspapers at the time, and only a black-bordered notice, fixed to the door of the Writers' House, announced the death of the poet Aleksandr Blok.

The same day, at about six o'clock in the evening, a short funeral service was held according to the Russian custom. There were a dozen of us gathered around his death-bed. Almost bald, his beard dark and temples white, thin, his face ravaged by suffering, he was unrecognizable. In the bare room Lyuba and Madame Kublitskaya were weeping.

And three days later, on a beautiful sunny day, Petersburg paid him a last homage. More than two hundred people followed the cortège. The open coffin was carried to the Smolensky cemetery by Bely, Pyast and other friends. There were no speeches.

We all felt it was the end of a life, the end of a city, the end of a world. The young people who surrounded the coffin understood that, for them, this day might be a beginning. As Blok and his contemporaries had been 'the children of the terrible years', so we would become 'the children of Aleksandr Blok'. Several months later, nothing would remain of this period of Russian life. Some had fled, some had been expelled, others, banned, were in hiding. A new era was on its way.

A new city would be born, with skyscrapers, housing estates, vast stadiums, culture parks, monuments to heroes of the revolution, a city of other struggles, other forces, other hopes, a city which even had to change its name.

Translator's Note

This is an informal biography. Berberova's notes are minimal, and I have added to them only where meaning would be obscured without further information. She has often conflated passages from Blok's letters and diaries. Readers looking for a more detailed study are referred to Avril Pyman's two-volume *Life of Aleksandr Blok* (Oxford University Press, 1979, 1980), to which I am much indebted. I should like to thank Joy Flint for her valuable advice on the translation, and Peter McCarey for his indispensable contribution to the translating of Blok's verse. I am also grateful to Nicola Bradbury, Peter France, Evan Mawdsley, Edwin Morgan and Avril Pyman for their suggestions.